Sandy 973 334-6064
Susan 781 856 - 1942

The Quotable Gambler

Books by Paul Lyons

Table Legs (a novel)
Going for Broke (a novel)
The Quotable Gambler (editor)

The Quotable Gambler

EDITED BY

PAUL LYONS

THE LYONS PRESS

For George and Amy with Aloha

Printed in the United States of America
Design by

10 9 8 7 6 5 4 3 2 1

The Library of Congress Cataloging-in-Publication Data is available on file.

Contents

Preface

In the literature on gambling there is a tradition of the author admitting at the outset that one motivation in writing the book is to sell enough copies to recover gambling losses. For instance, Jean de Prechac wrote in 1682, "The author, having lost at basset, managed to recoup by writing a book on the game that earned back for him most of what he had lost." S. W. Erdnase likewise wrote that his *The Expert at the Card Table* (1902) would not "make a fool wise, or curtail the annual crop of suckers; but whatever the result may be, if it sells it will accomplish the primary motive of the author, as he needs the money."

However far this little volume of gambling quotations goes toward repaying the losses I've sustained while gambling, I've much enjoyed the process of collecting them. Making my way through the various halls in which gambling expressions are to be found has been a way of intermixing labor and play. And that fact—that the pleasure of the doing can be itself a form of profit over and against calculations of gain or waste—is where I hope this book points: Whatever activities humanoids have been passionate about, the joy and play elements in the doing offer a measure of redemption. (Let me say at once, and have done with it, that where it is without joy gambling is a sickness.)

What a collection of quotations potentially offers is some distillation of the literature, a concert of voices that goes beyond what any single author could say on the subject. And gambling is an astonishingly vast and varied subject. The "itch for play," in Charles Cotton's memorable phrase (1674), the impulse to "make it interesting" or "sweeten the pot," seemingly pervades all times and places and all classes, from Gods who literally bet the Sky to mere mortals with nothing to gamble but themselves or parts of themselves. In short, gambling perhaps reveals the all-too-human capacity for a range of marvelously mixed behaviors, from the sublime to the stupid, as vividly as any activity.

If this book makes you more aware of the spirit of gamble, of why people have gambled and with what result, or why and how you yourself have gambled, it should add to the enjoyment you take in gambling, and even make you a better gambler. For my own part, in my various researches I have been cheered at the contemporaneity of expressions from the ancient gamblers, their ability to catch the smarts and sweats of skidding or the giddy highs of being on a roll. And I have been surprised, moved, delighted, and informed by the wit and (sometimes dubious) wisdom of contemporary gamblers. For me—a lifelong lover of books and sometime haunter of the Temples of Chance—the next best thing to gambling has been reading about others doing it.

Gambling, at its healthiest, is one way of activating the soul, nudging it from its hungry sleep. I'm speaking about gambling in its most reductive form: taking a chance. The act *of taking a chance is energizing. The* art *of taking a chance can lead to the sublime.*

STEPHEN DUNN
"Gambling: Remembrances and Assertions" (1993)

They gambled in the Garden of Eden, and they will again if there's another one.

RICHARD ALBERT CANFIELD (1855–1914)
quoted in Cy Rice, *Nick the Greek: King of Gamblers* (1969)

For Openers

In the beginning, everything was even money.

MIKE CARO
Mike Caro on Gambling (1984)

Looking for where the action is, one arrives at a romantic division of the world. On one side are the safe and silent places, the home, the well-regulated roles in business, industry and the professions; on the other are all those activities that generate expression, requiring the individual to lay himself on the line and place himself in jeopardy during a passing moment.

IRVING GOFFMAN
Where the Action Is (1967)

Odds are that if you're holding this book you already have some interest in gambling and gamblers, have some sense of the pervasiveness of gambling in human history. You have known for yourself the thin-ice thrills and dangers of "action" or "gamble," its defiance of restrictions, its shimmering chances for "ephemeral ennoblement" (as the sociologist Goffman calls it), and the seductive threat gamblers face of receiving a "status bloodbath" (Goffman) along with losing their bankrolls.

To gamble is to put something (a stake) at risk voluntarily, to court and cultivate "deep play"—play that has consequences, personal and material, within and against the narratives of a particular time, place, and culture. Everyone craves gamble in some form, for an infinite variety of reasons, many of them twisted, though all are connected to the desire for action that makes one feel more alive, that gets the juices going. Even if, especially if, it means playing with fire, the possibility of going in over one's head, head over heels.

"There's nothing wrong with sobriety in moderation," / wrote the poet John Ciardi, a gambler's thought to be sure, suggesting as it does that humans need to take proper precautions against the dullnesses in and around themselves, that they need to get drunk on something, anything—on wine or love or art or sport; in short, that the adult mind benefits from recess as much as the child's, that health requires play.

Play has been universally recognized by philosophers as a

vital and inescapable element of every human activity, profession, and enterprise. In *Homo Ludens* (1949), anthropologist Johan Huizinga argues that "You can deny, if you like, nearly all abstractions: justice, beauty, truth, goodness, mind, God. You can deny seriousness, but not play." For Huizinga, pure play is endlessly imaginative and free, and its spirit is impoverished when it becomes material, regulated, and competitive.

Among gamblers disposed to discuss such matters, most would agree that gamble includes Huizinga's sense of creative and joyful play, but would cringe at the idea of anything so wholesome, anything that so precludes the grime of the ruin factor, slings and arrows, and the dicey dream of bucking the odds.

But gamblers certainly could endorse Huizinga's semi-playful suggestions that humanoids be reclassified from *Homo sapiens* (man the knower) to *Homo ludens* (man the player).

Consider this book as a toast to *Homo ludens*.

Man does not live by bread alone. Man also does not live by art alone. Man needs his foolish dreams perhaps more than he needs anything else. For two reasons. He must forget the hardships and pain of life. He must forget that he must die. Also it can be argued that man's instinct to gamble is the only reason he is still not a monkey up in the trees.

> MARIO PUZO
> *Inside Las Vegas* (1976)

———•◆•———

It's my opinion that men will gamble as long as they have anything to put on a card. Gamble? That's nature. What's life itself? You never know what may turn up. The worst of it is that you can never tell exactly what kind of cards you are holding yourself. What's trumps?—this is the question. See? Any man will gamble if only given a chance. For anything or everything. You too—

> JOSEPH CONRAD
> *Victory* (1915)

———•◆•———

Man is a gaming animal.

> CHARLES LAMB
> "Mrs. Battle's Opinion of Whist," *Essays of Elia* (1832)

Gaming is a principle inherent in human nature.

> EDMUND BURKE
> speech before the House of Commons (1780)

———◆———

Man only plays when in the full meaning of the word he is a man, and *he is only completely a man when he plays.*

> FRIEDRICH SCHILLER
> "Aesthetic Letters and Essays" (1795)

———◆———

Play is so elementary a function of human life that culture is quite inconceivable without this element.

> HANS-GEORG GADAMER
> "The Relevance of the Beautiful" (1977)

———◆———

All the passions produce prodigies. A gambler is capable of watching and fasting, almost like a saint.

> SIMON WEIL
> quoted in Michael Herr, *The Big Room* (1986)

Life itself loses in interest when the highest stakes in the game of living, life itself, may not be risked.

SIGMUND FREUD
quoted in Larry Merchant, *The National Football Lottery* (1973)

———•◆•———

Everyone reaches out for risk. Everyone craves it. Some people may unconsciously seek out dangerous personal relationships. Rather than settle on a stable romance, they create an explosive situation in which they stalk a difficult reward while risking great pain. They are gamblers in the act of gambling.

MIKE CARO
Mike Caro on Gambling (1984)

———•◆•———

Games are nature's most beautiful creation. All animals play games, and the true Messianic vision of the brotherhood of creatures must be based on the idea of the game.

LEONARD COHEN
Beautiful Losers (1966)

Look high, look low, and we see that the gamblers actually form the majority of the world's inhabitants.

> JAMES RUNCIMAN
> *Side Lights* (1893)

———•◆•———

The urge to gamble is so universal and its practice so pleasurable, that I assume it must be evil.

> HEYWOOD BROUN
> quoted in Margaret Gronin Fisk, *The Gambler's Bible* (1976)

———•◆•———

A number of moralists condemn lotteries and refuse to see anything noble in the passion of the ordinary gambler. They judge gambling as some atheists judge religion, by its excesses.

> CHARLES LAMB
> *Essays of Elia* (1832)

———•◆•———

If you have never gambled, you are preciously rare and probably terminally boring.

> MICHAEL PAKENHAM
> review of Timothy L. O'Brien's *Bad Bet* (1998)

Games must be regarded not as conscious inventions, but as survivals from primitive conditions, under which they originated in magical rites and chiefly as means of divination.

STEWART CULIN (1858–1929)

The great archetypal activities of human society are all permeated with play from the start.

JOHAN HUIZINGA
Homo Ludens (1949)

The subject of gambling is all encompassing. It combines man's natural play instinct with his desire to know about his fate and his future . . . Fundamentally, it is nothing but an extension of the love of play which is so strong a force in man and which has never been fully tamed by sublimation through reason.

FRANZ ROSENTHAL
Gambling in Islam (1975)

Sure, there's tension and nerves. But you take the greatest dramatists in the world—Shakespeare, Shaw—they couldn't improve on the scripts you get in ballgames.

BOOKIE LEM BANKER
quoted in Larry Merchant, *The National Football Lottery* (1973)

————•◆•————

When a gambler picks up a pack of cards or a pair of dice he feels as though he has reduced an unmanageable world to a finite, visible and comprehensible size.

ANNABEL DAVIS-GOFF (EDITOR)
The Literary Companion to Gambling (1996)

————•◆•————

The typical gambler may not really understand the probabilistic nuances of the wheel or the dice, but such things seem a bit more tractable than, say, trying to raise a child in this lunatic society of ours.

ARTHUR S. REBER
The New Gambler's Bible (1996)

Games are significant in people's lives because in a game everything is clearly defined. You've got the rules and a given period of time in which to play; you've got boundaries and a beginning and an end. And whether you win, lose, or draw, at least something is sure. But life ain't like that at all.

JAMES JONES
quoted in George Plimpton (editor), *Writers at Work* (1988)

———— •◆• ————

The Watergate cover-up turned into a poker game on a national scale. It was, in an obvious sense, the biggest bluff that Nixon ever ran, the basis of which was that if the full weight and prestige of the Presidency were committed to the cover-up, Congress wouldn't "see."

DAVID SPANIER
Total Poker (1977)

There is no doubt that Khrushchev would have been a superb poker player. First, he is out to win. Second, like any good poker player, he plans ahead so that he can win the big pots. He likes to bluff, but he knows that if you bluff on the small pots and fail consistently to produce the cards, you must expect your opponent to call your bluff on the big pots.

> RICHARD NIXON
> *Six Crises* (1962)

———•◆•———

I have often wondered if the results of the Versailles Conferences following the First World War would have been different if Woodrow Wilson had been a poker player.

> CLYDE BRION DAVIS
> quoted in A. D. Livingston, *Poker Strategy and Winning Play* (1971)

———•◆•———

It is not absurd to try diagnosing a civilization in terms of the games that are especially popular there. In fact, if games are cultural factors and images, it follows that to a certain degree a civilization and its content may be characterized by its games.

> ROGER CAILLOIS
> *Man, Play, and Games* (1979)

We Egyptians are gamblers. Wherever Egyptians are gathered, you can be sure that sooner or later they'll start gambling. It's not that we want to win money or anything, we just like to gamble. We're lazy and we like to laugh. It's only when gambling that we are wide awake and working hard.

WAGUIH GHALI
Beer in the Snooker Club (1964)

Gambling in Australia. Where else in the world are jockeys more revered than musicians or scientists? Where else in the world are the people's clubs dependent for their existence on poker machines? Where else in the world is a famous racehorse stuffed and enshrined in a museum?

FRANK HARDY
The Four-Legged Lottery (1977)

Those who live in the midst of democratic fluctuations have always before their eyes the image of chance; and they end by liking all undertakings in which chance plays a part.

ALEXIS DE TOCQUEVILLE
Democracy in America (1848)

We [Americans] are a nation of gamblers—some cooly professional, some driven and compulsive, most casual but nonetheless fascinated.

DON ETHAN MILLER
The Book of Jargon (1981)

———•◆•———

Almost everybody gambled in the Old West. Prospectors and dance-hall girls, cattle barons and cowpokes, clergymen and gunfighters all gathered around gaming tables to wager their newly won fortunes—or their last possessions—on the turn of a card or the spin of a wheel . . . Gambling was a Western mania, the only amusement that could match the heady, speculative atmosphere of frontier life itself.

TIME-LIFE BOOKS
The Gamblers (1978)

———•◆•———

Judged by the dollars spent, gambling is now more popular in America than baseball, the movies, and Disneyland—*combined.*

TIMOTHY L. O'BRIEN
Bad Bet (1998)

Bets of robes, blankets, coins, and so forth were piled in the middle. Anyone could bet on a team, even women. Women also had their betting games, which could last for a few hours or several days. All bets had to be absolutely matched. . . . All gambling required good sportsmanship. It was shameful for pool losers to grieve. They would get no sympathy.

> MOURNING DOVE
> *Mourning Dove: A Salishan Autobiography,* edited by Jay Miller (1991)

The rulers of the country genuinely believed that betting eliminated strikes. Men had to work in order to gamble.

> MICHAEL ONDAATJE
> *Running in the Family* (1982)

I am sorry I have not learned to play at cards. It is very useful in life: it generates kindness and consolidates society.

> SAMUEL JOHNSON
> quoted in James Boswell, *Journal of a Tour to the Hebrides* (1739)

Playing cards is so popular among Rotumans that one might be forgiven for thinking they invented it . . . Sometimes, during the *av mane'a* season, a whole village may spend a day playing cards; if there is a visiting group, card-playing turns everyone into a clown of one kind or another.

> VILSONI HERENIKO
> *Woven Clowns* (1995)

———◆———

The Jewish nervous system seems to require more action than the Christian.

> NICK "THE GREEK" DANDALOS
> quoted in Cy Rice, *Nick the Greek: King of Gamblers* (1969)

———◆———

Only if a Jew won money from a Gentile was it not looked upon as theft.

> L. J. LUDOVICI
> *The Itch for Play* (1962)

A person who plays *nard* [a precursor to backgammon] without accompanying gambling is like . . . one who uses the grease of pigs to anoint himself.

> Ibn 'Umar
> quoted in Franz Rosenthal, *Gambling in Islam* (1975)

———•◆•———

"For the true gambler, money is never an end in itself. It's a tool, like language or thought."

> Lancey
> in Ring Lardner Jr. and Terry Southern (screenwriters)
> *The Cincinnati Kid* (1965)

———•◆•———

As far as The Sky is concerned, money is just something for him to play with and dollars might as well be doughnuts as far as value goes with him.

> Damon Runyon
> "The Idylls of Miss Sarah Brown" (1947)

It is a cold ecstasy which deals with money not as meaning, value, depth or substance, but in the pure form of appearance or disappearance . . . Gambling is an organised catastrophic, apparitional form—a total metamorphosis.

> JEAN BAUDRILLIARD
> *Simulations* (1983)

———•◆•———

The guy who invented gambling was bright, but the guy who invented the chip was a genius.

> BIG JULIE
> quoted in Alvin Alvarez, *The Biggest Game in Town* (1983)

———•◆•———

This money was once, and therefore will be again, chips. She and the casinos both know that chips are a wonderful, pretty tool, and possess none of the stigma of dollars. Dollars translate too easily into hours or houses or cars or sex or food or everything, and so losing a dollar is a much more tangible experience than parting with a chip, an object that looks more like a midway consolation token than a medium of exchange.

> JOHN O'BRIEN
> *Leaving Las Vegas* (1990)

Gambling had invested money with the quality of a medium necessary to the condition of life. It was not that I wanted to *do* anything with it, any more than I wanted to *do* something with oxygen or sunlight; it was simply that cash had become the element I needed for my personal evolution.

> JACK RICHARDSON
> *Memoir of a Gambler* (1979)

———•◆•———

It is not as destructive as war or as boring as pornography. It is not as immoral as business or as suicidal as watching television. And the percentages are better than religion.

> MARIO PUZO
> *Inside Las Vegas* (1976)

———•◆•———

Life is the folly of rolling the dice without another thought— the insistence on a state of grace, or lack of consequences. To worry about consequences is the beginning of greed and anguish. The latter comes from the former: it's the trembling produced by chance.

> GEORGES BATAILLE
> *Guilty* (1961)
> translated by Bruce Boone

Gambling is good for you . . . Any activity such as gambling, which the human race has pursued since man began to walk upright, and perhaps even before then, which has been popular in virtually all societies throughout history . . . has got to have a lot going for it.

DAVID SPANIER
Easy Money: Inside the Gambler's Mind (1987)

———•◆•———

The billiard table is better than the doctors. I walk not less than ten miles with a cue in my hand, and the walking is not the whole of the exercise, nor the most health-giving part of it. I think, through the multitude of positions and attitudes, it brings every muscle into play and exercises them all.

MARK TWAIN (1835–1910)

———•◆•———

Pool has been offered as a recreation in asylums for about 150 years. Alas, more people have been driven crazy by pool during that time than have been cured by it.

MIKE SHAMOS
Pool: History, Strategies, and Legends (1994)

When the world is wrong, hardly to be endured, I shall return to Thurston's Hall and there smoke a pipe among the connoisseurs of top and side.

J. B. PRIESTLEY
"At Thurstson's" (1932)

When it seemed to me after a long illness that death was close at hand, I found no little solace in playing constantly at dice.

GEROLAMO CARDANO
The Book on Games of Chance (c. 1520)

"Let me tell you, there's no better medicine than a friendly card game for sloughing off the cares of the workaday world."

"It's relaxing," Stone said. "It helps you get your mind off things."

"Precisely," Flower said. "It helps to open the spirit to other possibilities, to wipe the slate clean."

PAUL AUSTER
The Music of Chance (1990)

Gambling . . . helped me more than analysis. I suffered from depression—I was so entwined with my inner world I never had a chance to enjoy myself. For me, activity was the answer. I took up gambling *after* I finished with psychoanalysis, and the depressions never returned.

> MICKEY APPLEMAN
> quoted in Alvin Alvarez, *The Biggest Game in Town* (1983)

———•◆•———

When I played pool I was like a good psychiatrist. I cured 'em all of all their daydreams and delusions.

> MINNESOTA FATS
> quoted in Jon Bradshaw, *Fast Company* (1975)

———•◆•———

Gambling is a way of buying hope on credit.

> ALAN WYKES
> *The Complete Illustrated Guide to Gambling* (1964)

———•◆•———

Gaming itself . . . will only end when human nature has changed completely and there are no more bets to win.

> HAROLD S. SMITH SR. WITH JOHN WESLEY NOBLE
> *I Want to Quit Winners* (1961)

What, then, is the right way of living? Life must be lived as play, playing certain games, making sacrifices, singing and dancing, and then a man will be able to propitiate the gods, and defend himself against his enemies, and win in the contest.

PLATO (C. 427–347 B.C.)
"Laws"

And games are stories too, not just swallowers of time, or buds without fruit. Games, as played out stories, also define our life.

PATRICIA GRACE
Potiki (1986)

2

The Gifts of Gamble

*He loved gambling for its own sake, like moralists love virtue
for its own sake.*

> GEORGE DEVOL
> on "Canada" Bill Jones
> *Forty Years a Gambler on the Mississippi* (1892)

*He let his heart experience the fine old ecstasy of the gambler's
life: his dedicated life, lived at the edge of the world and partly
in dream, where polished balls spun across a brilliant green,
where his skill shone in a room beneath layers of smoke.*

> WALTER TEVIS
> *The Color of Money* (1984)

I received a reasonably good undergraduate education in gambling (with a minor in one pocket) at the Guys and Dolls poolroom over a Woolworth's on the corner of Seventy-Ninth Street and Broadway. There was the obligatory NO GAMBLING sign right behind the action table, above which thick cigar smoke swirled in triangular shafts of light. Against the walls sweaters and stakehorses held side action, and sometimes after hours the houseman locked the front door and played all-night craps games on the billiard tables, and uptown guys would fade and sass the whole place, yelling, "Eight skate and donate," or, "If I don't six there ain't no Jesus."

What I loved about Guys and Dolls, the occasional lumps aside, were the things I have loved about many places where I've gambled since. These things I consider "gifts of gamble": the sweet anticipation of risk; the click of the pool balls or muted voices around a smoky table as you approach; the disembodied clarity of being in deadly stroke, pocket mouths opening wide; the loyalties and streaky alliances among side bettors; characters known primarily by their racehorselike gambling names (Silverheart, Oil Can, Cheesecake, Madame Mustache, Titanic); weasel-faced pontiffs of the morning line and doctors and garish-dressing dealers in fedoras rubbing shoulders in a free-form community of people who give each other action (when there are no pigeons to be had); the delicate and exacting art of the game played well.

And as much as anything I have loved the stories—most of which you'd bet have little more relation to reality than Hans Christian Andersen's—and the magnificent wit and energy and rawness of speech in that poolroom. There were guys up there whose trash talk and schooling of an opponent could make your ribs bust with laughter. I've sometimes wondered why career gamblers are, on the whole, so much sharper and livelier in their repartee than the scholars, hacks, and pundits whose business it is to work with words. A large part of it must be the lack of restraint, and a willingness to gamble on expression. "Words is like the spots on dice: no matter how y fumbles em, there's time when they jes won't come," says a character in Jean Toomer's *Cane,* brilliantly connecting the chance factor in off-the-cuff improvisational speech to the dance of dice, and suggesting the small victory in finding adequate eloquence, feeling the words rush sometimes and letting speech ride.

I'm talking about irresponsible happiness. And that's what gambling is to some degree. And yet it is more than that. It is the gambling instinct in man that lifted him up the evolutionary scale, that has led to scientific progress. Why the hell should anyone want to get to the moon?

MARIO PUZO
Inside Las Vegas (1976)

———•◆•———

The exhilaration of this form of economic existence is beyond my power to describe.

NICK "THE GREEK" DANDALOS
quoted in Jon Bradshaw, *Fast Company* (1975)

———•◆•———

Gamblers play just as lovers make love and drunkards drink—blindly and of necessity, under domination of an irresistible force.

ANATOLE FRANCE
The Garden of Epicurus (1926)
translated by Alfred Allinson

———•◆•———

We gamble because we can't help ourselves. We love it.

TIMOTHY L. O'BRIEN
Bad Bet (1998)

Give him the same amount of money every morning that he is likely to win during the day's play on condition that he does not gamble, and you will make him thoroughly unhappy. It will perhaps be said that he only cares about the fun of gambling and not about his winnings. But make him play for nothing; he will not get any excitement out of it at all and will merely be bored. This means that he is not looking for entertainment alone . . . He must grow excited and fool himself into believing that he would be delighted to win the money that he would hate to be given to him on the condition that he does not gamble.

BLAISE PASCAL
Pensées (1670)
translated by Martin Turnell

———•◆•———

Taking the cubes in hand and making them bounce to my bidding produces pure passion in me. I know all the risks inherent in games of chance and that nothing I can do can remove those risks. Yet I go for the big money, often so big it's more than I can afford to lose. And I hope to win. I must and do give complete credence to seemingly nebulous things like hunches, luck and extrasensory perception.

HAROLD S. SMITH SR. WITH JOHN WESLEY NOBLE
I Want to Quit Winners (1961)

If there was no action around, he would play solitaire—and bet against himself.

GROUCHO MARX (1891–1977)
on his brother Chico

———•◆•———

Gambling releases us from the real world. We are isolated. There is no outside, no past or future, only here and now . . . We suspend ourselves at a comfortable level of arousal . . . There's no feeling like the one when our money hits the table.

LANCE HUMBLE, PH.D., AND CARL COOPER, PH.D.
The World's Greatest Blackjack Book (1980)

———•◆•———

People's hobbies are more their measure than are their jobs. Never mind what they are forced to do, like fight wars or make a living or embrace the king's religion. What do they *choose* to do in their spare time, if they have any?

ROBERT BYRNE
Byrne's Book of Great Pool Stories (1995)

Each match is a world unto itself, a particular burst of form.

> CLIFFORD GEERTZ
> "Deep Play: Notes on the Balinese Cockfight" (1972)

———— •◆• ————

Fatefulness brings the individual into a very special relationship to time, and serious action brings him there voluntarily. He must arrange to be in a position to let go, and then do so . . . He must give himself up to the certain rapid resolution of an uncertain outcome. And he must give himself up to fate in this way when he could avoid it at reasonable cost. He must have "gamble."

> IRVING GOFFMAN
> *Where the Action Is* (1967)

———— •◆• ————

Games always cover something deep and intense, else there would be no excitement in them, no pleasure, no power to stir us.

> ANTOINE DE SAINT-EXUPÉRY
> *Airman's Odyssey* (1942)
> translated by Lewis Galantiere

Play . . . allows you to positively glimpse the giddy seductiveness of chance.

> GEORGES BATAILLE
> *Guilty* (1961)
> translated by Bruce Boone

———•◆•———

A true gambler played because he loved the thrill he had on the turn of a card, because it tested his ability to out-wit and out-guess the other person.

> POKER ALICE
> quoted in Nolie Mumey, *Poker Alice* (1951)

———•◆•———

Lucinda feels . . . the familiar electric ecstasy, beyond salvation and uncaring. She looks at no one. She plays with inspired recklessness. She feels she can control the game with her will.

> LAURA JONES (SCREENWRITER)
> of Peter Cary, *Oscar and Lucinda* (1998)

He tried to explain gambling by saying that it was the difference between walking through an abandoned orchard with a gun and a dog, looking for grouse, and just walking.

CRAIG NOVA
"Another Drunk Gambler" (1986)

———◆——

It was a joy to see the money move at a sedate pace back and forth across the table, as if it had a life of its own, or was reacting to my will, or the dealer's, or even the magic in the cards.

FREDRICK BARTHELME
Bob the Gambler (1997)

———◆——

He knew that the chief thing was gambling for its own sake—*le jeu pour le jeu.*

SIGMUND FREUD
"Dostoevsky and Parricide" (1928)

———◆——

I would rather play poker with five or six experts than to eat.

POKER ALICE
quoted in Nolie Mumey, *Poker Alice* (1951)

I've often thought, If I got really hungry for a good milk shake, how much would I pay for one? People will pay a hundred dollars for a bottle of wine; to me that's not worth it. But I'm not going to say it is foolish or wrong to spend that kind of money, if that's what you want. So if a guy wants to bet twenty or thirty thousand dollars in a poker game, that is his privilege.

> JACK BINON
> quoted in Alvin Alvarez, *The Biggest Game in Town* (1983)

———◆———

I have denounced everything but wine.
I have foresworn everything but gambling.

> PERSIAN VERSES
> quoted in Franz Rosenthal, *Gambling in Islam* (1975)

———◆———

Wine loved I deeply, dice dearly.

> WILLIAM SHAKESPEARE
> *King Lear* (1606)

———◆———

They clinked their glasses to the glorious game of "Nap," lighted cigars, and fell to shuffling and dealing the cards.

> JACK LONDON
> *The Sea Wolf* (1904)

They drank the health of the Queen of Hearts and of the Queen of Diamonds.

> JAMES JOYCE
> "After the Race" (1914)

———————•◆•———————

He discovered that a betting man with an honest dollar to back his judgement on a subject was equal to anyone, anywhere, any time, and that from time immemorial there had been men who would bet, rich men with poor, smart men with stupid men, black men with white men. The size of a man's bet was not a significant factor, nor what he bet on, nor how he bet. It was the idea of a man backing his judgement with something of value and taking the chance of losing.

> RICHARD JESSUP
> *The Cincinnati Kid* (1963)

———————•◆•———————

He speaks the language of the game he plays at, better than the language of his country.

> CHARLES COTTON
> *The Compleate Gamester* (1674)

"I'll take nine to eight and everybody in the state of Washington can bet. The hundred-dollar window is open."

> BUCKTOOTH
> quoted in David McCumber, *Off the Rail* (1996)

———————•◆•———————

The bank is open, the sky is the limit.

> POKER ALICE
> quoted in Nolie Mumey, *Poker Alice* (1951)

———————•◆•———————

"What are the stakes like?" I asked.
   "Try the top sirloin," he said dryly.

> DICK MILES
> "Lowball in a Time Capsule" (1970)

———————•◆•———————

I'm a gambler. I'll always be one. I couldn't be anything else. So, my life will always be full of wins and losses. I wouldn't have it any other way. It's exciting. There's never been a dull moment in my life.

> DOYLE BRUNSON
> *How I Made $1,000,000 Playing Poker* (1979)

"That cue has radar and microcircuits in its tip. With a cue like that a man can lay in bed and send the cue stick out on Saturday nights. 'Bring in five hundred, Balabushka' is what you say."

WALTER TEVIS
The Color of Money (1984)

———•◆•———

I've never seen anyone grow humpbacked carrying away the money they won from me.

POKER ALICE
quoted in Nolie Mumey, *Poker Alice* (1951)

———•◆•———

"I love it when they hit. You know the sound when they hit? That dinghy sound, it's like faster, and contained somehow? That's a great sound. Happens a fraction of a second before you know what you've hit, before you figure it out."

"The machine's thinking it wants to surprise you," I said.

FRED BARTHELME
Bob the Gambler (1997)

"Get a fuckin heart transplant and come back and play me."
"Get a cash transplant and we'll play tonight," Tony said.

> DAVID MCCUMBER
> *Off the Rail* (1996)

———•◆•———

I'd go to the moon if they were anteing high enough.

> BOBBY BALDWIN, WORLD-CHAMPION POKER PLAYER
> quoted in Alvin Alvarez, *The Biggest Game in Town* (1983)

———•◆•———

A pair of six-shooters beats a pair of sixes.

> BELLE STARR (1877)
> quoted in Greg Stebbin and Terry Hall, *Cowboy Wisdom* (1995)

———•◆•———

Look at that guy—can't run six balls and he's president of the United States.

> JOHNNY IRISH, POOL HUSTLER
> on Richard Nixon
> quoted in Dan McGoorty and Robert Byrne, *McGoorty* (1972)

I must complain the cards are ill shuffled till I have a good hand.

> JONATHAN SWIFT
> "Thoughts on Various Subjects" (1728)

———•◆•———

"Lemon shuffles like my mother when she deals Go Fish to my ten-year-old nephew," Billy said.

> WILLIAM KENNEDY
> *Billy Phelan's Greatest Game* (1978)

———•◆•———

"Irv, you're the only Jew I know took Germany plus the points."

> DAVID LEVIEN AND BRIAN KOPPLEMAN (SCREENWRITERS)
> *Rounders* (1998)

———•◆•———

A priest rebuked a gambler for the time he wasted at play. "Yes," replied the latter, "there is a lot of time lost in shuffling the cards."

> CHARLES WILLIAM HECKETHORN (ROUGE ET NOIR)
> *The Gambling World* (1898)

"If I could play this game like you, I'd rent the chair I'm sitting in for a year . . . I'm not lying. I wouldn't need a house, car, job or a friend. This chair would be my only possession."

> JACK RICHARDSON
> *Memoir of a Gambler* (1979)

———•◆•———

I started playing a young farmer in his 20s and stuck him up for like $4 and he ran like a deer. He told me I was a pretty good pool player but he said there was no way I could beat a friend of his who he called Ole Sauerkraut.

> MINNESOTA FATS WITH TOM FOX
> *The Great Bank Shot and Other Great Robberies* (1966)

———•◆•———

He couldn't play; he *wouldn't* play anybody good. We used to stand around helpless with laughter when he told his stories about winning millions in India or in the Depression or wherever or whenever.

> DAN DiLIBERTO
> on Fats
> quoted in Dan McGoorty and Robert Byrne, *McGoorty* (1972)

The more I hang around you pool hall imbeciles, the more I realize I'm the most intelligent man I know. I could spot Einstein the ten ball.

> MINNESOTA FATS
> quoted in Jon Bradshaw, *Fast Company* (1975)

———•◆•———

Beating them three weeks in a row in Las Vegas is like going into the lion's den and coming out with meat under both arms.

> LARRY MERCHANT
> *The National Football Lottery* (1973)

———•◆•———

"You've never seen me welch on a bet," Bones pleaded. "No, I never did," said Monty thoughtfully. "But you used to have a farm. Do you have one now?"

> HERBERT O. YARDLEY
> *The Education of a Poker Player* (1957)

———•◆•———

All of us who gamble are, importantly, fellow gamblers.

> STEPHEN DUNN
> "Gambling: Remembrances and Assertions" (1993)

In poker one has cards, chips, and conversation.

> JOHN MCDONALD
> *Strategy in Poker, Business, and War* (1950)

———— •◆• ————

A gambler's acquaintance is readily made and easily kept—provided you gamble too.

> EDWARD BULWER-LYTTON
> *Pelham* (1828)

———— •◆• ————

In spite of the apparent impersonality of the operation, strangers at the same table find that a slight camaraderie is generated by joint and mutually visible exposure to fate.

> IRVING GOFFMAN
> *Where the Action Is* (1967)

———— •◆• ————

People who never saw each other fifteen minutes before, and will never see each other again after fifteen minutes more, are caught up in a frenzy of laughter and enthusiasm, or life.

> LARRY MERCHANT
> *The National Football Lottery* (1973)

The unrehearsed "rapport" of the entire table, combined with the winning Eleven, has turned the sound of the table to the booming, raucous laughter of immense happiness! A bond of winning togetherness has been established. *Nobody* will fail in this bond. It will only become stronger. A deafening but perfectly in-unison "Show it to me" has come from the entire table . . . The whole table has picked up the rapid chant and people are placing their bets, chanting all the time.

JOSEPH WALSH (SCREENWRITER)
California Split (1973)

In moments of relaxation, when the ship lay an anchor and there was nothing to do, the two white men seated on one side of the skylight and the two brown on the other, with a large bottle of Holland's gin between them, would endeavor to rook each other at cards.

LOUIS BECKE
South Seas Supercargo (1890)

"When I play with you for a sum I tell you in effect I'll do my best to spoil your diversion, to send you home with your head disturb'd, your pocket light and your heart heavy. And is there not a great deal of friendship in this profession?"

JEREMY COLLIER
"An Essay on Gaming in a Dialogue between Callimachus and Dolomedes" (1713)

———•◆•———

And we spit on the wager, which I taught him, and we shake on the wager, which he taught me. And we both know that's that. He stands, takes a last drag off his butt, and says "Good night, Stevie," pretty near pleasantly . . . the whole thing's moved to another level: it's not what we'd call an intellectual exercise anymore, it's a wager, and further talk would only desecrate it. From this point on there'll just be the playing of the game, the run to the wire, with one of us ending up a winner and the other a loser.

CALEB CARR
The Angel of Darkness (1997)

He's a good enough player to know that I know what he's thinkin', just like he knows what I'm thinkin'. Hell, we're environment, we know each other like hills and streams.

> Pug Pearson
> quoted in Jon Bradshaw, *Fast Company* (1975)

———•◆•———

It is said that the Earl of Sandwich invented that most common item of food that bears his name so that he could manage to eat without leaving the gambling table.

> Lyn Barrow
> *Compulsion* (1969)

———•◆•———

"Gambling is an art form," he said to me. "Some people gamble because they think there is money in it. Yes, there is money in it when you are lucky. But then the meaning of the game is distorted."

> Carlos Bulosan
> *America Is in the Heart* (1943)

Gambling was his life. He played incessantly, passionately, joyfully, and always for high stakes; not as a business or a profession, but as truly devoted monks must pray . . . as a kind of prolonged ecstasy.

NICK "THE GREEK" DANDALOS
quoted in Ted Thackrey Jr., *Gambling Secrets of Nick the Greek* (1968)

———•◆•———

Eddie loved to play pool. There was a kind of power, a kind of brilliant co-ordination of mind and of skill, that could give him as much pleasure, as much delight in himself and in the things that he did, as anything else in the world. Some men never feel this way about anything.

WALTER TEVIS
The Hustler (1959)

———•◆•———

"I'm down to my last buck, pal. Wanna split a bet with me?"

"On which horse?"

"I don't care."

BRENDAN BOYD
Racing Days (1987)

3

"It's Bad Luck to Be Superstitious"

Can one even as much as touch a gaming table without becoming immediately infected with superstition?

> FYODOR DOSTOEVSKY
> *The Gambler* (1867)
> translated by Victor Terras

"Hold up, Arm," he would plead,
Kissing his rosary once for help
With the faders sweating it out and—
Zing!—there it was—Little Joe or Eighter from
  Decatur
Double-trey the hard way, Dice be Nice,
When you get a hunch bet a bunch

> NELSON ALGREN
> "Epitaph for the Man with
> the Golden Arm" (1960)

The title for this section is a bit of advice from maestro kibbitzer Vinnie Schamasky, given freely and frequently in the House of Backgammon that used to be above the OTB on Seventy-Second Street, just off Broadway. To my knowledge Vinnie's perfectly golden advice never persuaded one person in the joint to abandon their superstitious ways.

To stand by a craps table and watch the delicate rituals with which shooters pick up the dice, blow on them, and chant particular "sweet talk" expressions believed to bring about a hard eight, to watch poker players touch rings with four-leaf clovers or horseshoes on them or rub rabbit's foot key chains before looking at their hole card, is to apprehend a connection between our age of extreme materialism (epitomized by the postmodern casino) and that magic period just before the dawn of civilization when everything looked for all the world like an omen, and our hairier precursors rolled bones to divine the will of the Gods.

Nearly every gambler I have ever known has been superstitious to some degree, possessed of systems and rituals, prone to switch rolling hands to break a disastrous dice streak, not above calling on the Gods ("Help, Backgammon Gods, it's your friend Slim").

I must confess that for a period of my life I would not wash a lucky pair of pants until I lost in them, and carried an 1898 silver dollar worth all of three bucks. I've known scholars and scientists of gambling who professed not to give credence to anything outside the so-called laws of probability, who still believed that a particular hat brought them luck, and who wouldn't play without it. A gifted eight-ball player at the Guys and Dolls poolroom never appeared without wearing two hats, one on top of the other. No doubt such practices have their roots in egocentric thinking—the desire to see ourselves as factors in the scheme of things just out of sight—and the real, unacceptable fear is that of a wholly impersonal universe in which the charm or the lucky pants or that dollar bill safety-pinned to your underwear or the hat (or hats) don't make a damn difference, that there is no magic, at least for us. And yet, with a gambler's rechargeable optimism, I say go on wearing that hat of yours and believing it a conduit to luck, whatever the computer odds against, whatever the evidence to the contrary.

When it comes to Luck, reader, look into your heart, and what are you but an atheist and a believer too?

———— •◆• ————

I am a reasonable American, registered to vote, sitting at the blackjack table, losing, with a $2 bill safety-pinned to the front of my underpants.

> EDWARD ALLEN
> "Penny Ante" (1992)

———— •◆• ————

One man I know likes all the traffic lights to be green when he drives to a game, so he can get the feeling of everything going right for him.

> DAVID SPANIER
> *Total Poker* (1977)

The next morning before leaving to play, I put on some Old Spice after-shave lotion. My next session was a dramatic winner. For the next several weeks I doused myself with this lotion without fail before playing. If I went out the door, and remembered that I'd forgotten the after-shave lotion, I'd return for it. Sure, we're scientists, but I guess certain superstitions creep in periodically.

KEN USTON
Two Books on Blackjack (1979)

All gamblers look for signs, and I was given an appropriate one that first week when a filling from one of my molars popped out.

BILL BARICH
Laughing in the Hills (1980)

Each of us naturally tries to achieve his own personal harbinger of luck. One eccentric character named Blanchard won a big coup at Monte Carlo after a passing pigeon had soiled his hat. After that he went every season and strolled around waiting for another pigeon.

ALAN WYKES
The Complete Illustrated Guide to Gambling (1964)

'Tis not a ridiculous devotion, to say a Prayer before a game at tables?

SIR THOMAS BROWNE
Religio Medici (1642)

———•◆•———

Chronic numbers players . . . see clues to their fortune in the most minute and insignificant phenomena, in clouds, on passing trucks and subway cars, in creams, comic strips, the shape of dog-luck fouled on pavements.

RALPH ELLISON
Invisible Man (1952)

———•◆•———

Many gamblers think they've been singled out by fate as a target for cruel jokes. They feel they alone in all the universe are being tortured, experimented upon by some unknown force.

MIKE CARO
Mike Caro on Gambling (1984)

"You will see players talking to the dice, kissing the dice, fixing the dice in all sorts of ways. Some will rub their hands on the table as if to rub off some magic onto themselves. Still others will pray and make incantations. It comes with the territory of craps. It comes with the country. So when in another country I follow the customs of the country."

THE CAPTAIN
quoted in Frank Scoblete
Beat the Craps Out of the Casinos (1991)

If you're playing blackjack, especially when it's going particularly well or badly, every blip in the environment thrives with meaning. You think Alanis Morissette on the sound system is a jinx, that the number of ice cubes in your glass brings bad luck.

FREDRICK AND STEVEN BARTHLEME
"Good Losers" (1999)

When a gambler walks around his chair to change his luck he is marking out a circle to keep out the evil spirits, and when he blows on the dice he is symbolically blowing life into a dying object.

J. PHILIP JONES
Gambling Yesterday and Today (1973)

The player finds special significance in all kinds of phenomena, encounters, and omens, which he imagines to be forebodings of good or bad luck. He looks for talismans that will protect him most efficaciously.

Roger Caillois
Man, Play, and Games (1979)

———•◆•———

Anyone who isn't superstitious hasn't played backgammon.

Phil Simborg
"Simborg's Laws of Backgammon" (1998)

———•◆•———

He talks to the dice or makes a system at roulette, imploring favor. He wears charms, tips beggars . . . all to seek the mystic rhythm of the universe and determine its future . . . On losing he is not only dejected; worse, his appeals ignored, he feels rejected. No one who is not a gambler knows the depths to which he is thrown by Fortune's refusal to give her love.

John McDonald
Strategy in Poker, Business, and War (1950)

I don't want to take any chips off the table . . . you know that's bad luck.

> JOSEPH WALSH (SCREENWRITER)
> *California Split* (1973)

———•◆•———

Numbers have souls, and you can't help but get involved with them in a personal way.

> PAUL AUSTER
> *The Music of Chance* (1990)

———•◆•———

The God delights in odd numbers.

> VIRGIL
> *Eclogues* (43–37 B.C.)

———•◆•———

This is the third time; I hope good luck lies in odd numbers . . . There is a divinity in odd numbers, either in nativity, chance, or death.

> SIR JOHN FALSTAFF
> in William Shakespeare
> *Merry Wives of Windsor* (1592)

How greatly have its sixes confused my mind, and how much anxiety have its fives forced down my throat.

> ANONYMOUS PERSIAN POET
> quoted in Franz Rosenthal, *Gambling in Islam* (1975)

———•◆•———

CHARLIE: Eleven! I won't even *accept* a Seven.
STICKMAN: Winner Seven.
CHARLIE: I *accept* it. I lied!
  (to dice)
    Faked you out!

> JOSEPH WALSH (SCREENWRITER)
> *California Split* (1973)

———•◆•———

Betting and gambling would lose half their attractiveness, did they not deceive us with the fancy that there may be an element of personal merit in our winnings. Our reason may be protest, but our self-love is credulous.

> ROBERT LYND
> *The Peal of Bells* (1925)

Particularly important . . . is to avoid putting on any article of clothing in which I have had a bad night in the past. Unfortunately, a too-strict observance of this rule always leads to a problem with shoes because I have only a limited number, and I've had terrible nights in every pair I own.

EDWARD ALLEN
"Penny Ante" (1992)

———— • ◆ • ————

I don't eat peanuts at the card table. There's no reason in the world eating peanuts should affect the outcome of the game, but it doesn't cost me anything to observe the taboo against it, so I observe it . . . When I lose a hand or two, I sometimes get up and walk around the chair.

DOYLE BRUNSON
How I Made $1,000,000 Playing Poker (1979)

———— • ◆ • ————

He nourished a conviction that there must be some logic lurking somewhere in the results of chance.

JOSEPH CONRAD
"The End of the Tether" (1899)

"You sitting next to me in Las Vegas isn't going to affect what happens in San Francisco," I said, not at all certain that this was really so.

> JACK RICHARDSON
> *Memoir of a Gambler* (1979)

———◆———

A simple method of making a man lose is to wait until he has thrown a used matchstick into the ashtray, and then put another crosswise over it. His luck is thus crossed out.

> E. & M. RADFORD
> *Encyclopaedia of Superstitions* (1942)

———◆———

A gambler's instinct comprehends relations between events that are perhaps too subtle for ordinary modes of observation. It is this instinct on which his survival is based, for if he ignores it and, while feeling disconnected from propitious flows and patterns, continues stubbornly to force a return of the good feeling he had about himself, he becomes nothing but an item of desperation, someone doomed to be unloved by fortune and destroyed by mathematics.

> JACK RICHARDSON
> *Memoir of a Gambler* (1979)

You use a slot or a game that is strictly sucker action to get a quick look at the particular cycle [of luck] that you are playing in.

NICK "THE GREEK" DANDALOS
quoted in Ted Thackrey Jr., *Gambling Secrets of Nick the Greek* (1968)

———— • ◆ • ————

I'm naturally paranoid. When I play cards with my kids I always cut the deck . . . All gamblers are paranoid, though they call it superstition.

MARIO PUZO
Inside Las Vegas (1976)

———— • ◆ • ————

It is especially in games of chance that the weakness of the human mind and its tendency toward superstition manifest themselves . . . And it is much the same for people's behavior in all those areas of life where chance plays a role.

PIERRE REMOND DE MONTMORT
Essai d'analyse sur les jeux de hasard (1713)

The cards knew about his wish and deliberately gave him bad hands to irritate him. He pretended that he was quite indifferent to his hands and tried to avoid turning up the box as long as possible. On the rare occasion he could deceive the cards this way, but usually they guessed and, when he did resort to opening the box, three sixes grinned at him and the king of spades, brought along for company, smiled sullenly.

LEONID ANDREEV
"The Grand Slam" (1899)

———•◆•———

Astrologers make claims for themselves; yet I have never seen an astrologer who was lucky at gambling, nor were those lucky who took their advice.

GEROLAMO CARDANO
The Book on Games of Chance (c. 1520)

———•◆•———

"I dreamed a big catfish jumped off the place and bit me, Daddy. Madame Zora gives five-fourteen for fish."

Daddy laughed. "That's a good dream, Sugar. I'll put a dollar on it."

Daddy said that of all the family my dreams hit the most.

LOUISE M. MERIWETHER
Daddy Was a Numbers Runner (1970)

We explore ourselves and others mercilessly, greedily, for the smallest sign that God has touched us more or less than He has touched them . . . 'Do me a big favour, just this once, God!' implores a gambler in an American musical.

L. J. LUDOVICI
The Itch for Play (1962)

———•◆•———

With the perverse logic of the true degenerate gambler he figured God was testing his faith.

MARIO PUZO
Inside Las Vegas (1976)

———•◆•———

The gambler likes to think of a divinity at his shoulder ready at any moment to intervene in his favour. The loser can lose without shame or damage to self-respect because he imagines that the inscrutable divinity standing over him has only temporarily withheld favour.

L. J. LUDOVICI
The Itch for Play (1962)

Based as it is on an organized rejection of all reason as a factor, it removes its devotees into a positive atmosphere of miracle, and generates an emotional excitement than inhibits those checks which reason more or less contrives to place on emotional extravagances.

JOHN A. HOBSON, MORAL PHILOSOPHER (1858–1940)

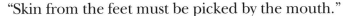

"Skin from the feet must be picked by the mouth."

"This is a well-known fact," Mrs. Nackla said. "This morning my husband tried to pick some skin from my feet which I have been saving for my son Hamo's big game tomorrow. I thought it was the dog licking my feet."

"You can laugh," Jameel said. "Assam the Turk swears he buys skin from a local skin-giver, and he's winning like anything."

So I took my shoes and stockings off, and Jameel rubbed his mouth against my soles for luck.

WAGUIH GHALI
Beer in the Snooker Club (1964)

Every gambler gives the impression of a man who has signed a contract with Fate, stipulating that persistence must be rewarded. With that imaginary contract in his pocket, he is beyond the reach of all logical objection and argument.

EDMUND BERGLER
The Psychology of Gambling (1958)

———◆———

The people who run the casinos are tough and smart in so many ways, but they belong in the Dark Ages . . . They explain the phenomena of their world the way the ancient astrologers did. They really believe that dice get hot.

EDWARD O. THORP
quoted in Edward Reid and Ovid Demaris, *The Green Felt Jungle* (1965)

———◆———

Nothing is so unpredictable as a throw of the dice, and yet every man who plays often will at some time or other make a venus-cast: now and then indeed he will make it twice and even thrice is succession. Are we going to be so feeble-minded then as to aver that such a thing happened by the personal intervention of Venus rather than by pure luck?

CICERO (106–43 B.C.)
De Divinatione

To dream that you hear a clock strike, if it strikes loud and plain, is a good dream to play the number of times you hear it strike first, more especially in the night lottery. If it appears to strike very fast, the sooner will the number be drawn first.

OLD AUNT DINAH'S POLICY DREAM BOOK (1830s)

"Well, some play by hunches, dreams, or numbers on a car or transfer ticket. Some go to Spiritualists. They are obtained for the most part, though, from dreams and hunches. You watch the 'book' your dream falls in most and play in that 'book.' Some people are lucky and some are not. Some people believe in burning incenses for good luck. They claim it gives them success. My dreams are good in the Harlem and the Bronx."

ST. CLAIR DRAKE AND HORACE CLAYTON
NUMBERS PLAYER
quoted in *Black Metropolis* (1945)

Not leads, omens.

AXEL FREED
on halftime scores
in James Toback (screenwriter)
The Gambler (1974)

4

Luck

Nobody ever knows why one person is lucky and another unlucky.

> D. H. LAWRENCE
> "The Rocking-Horse Winner" (1926)

The chief factor in the gambling habit is the belief in luck; and this belief is apparently traceable, at least in its elements, to a stage in human evolution antedating the predatory culture.

> THORSTEIN VEBLEN
> *The Theory of the Working Class* (1899)

In the glittering Land of the Short Run, which most recreational gamblers visit on junkets, Luck reigns supreme. It is happiness—in German *luck* and *happiness* are the same word—and without a longing for it there would be none of that delicious tingling as you drop a dollar in the slot and crank the lever. If three cherries click into place you take the family out for surf and turf. Otherwise you join the people's buffet line (open twenty-four hours) for generous helpings of marbled Jell-O.

In the Tenements of the Long Run, where philosophers and degenerate gamblers reside, Luck shimmers just out of sight like religion, a question for belief or skepticism ("come-line" or "don't pass" betting). For theists of Luck, it is a kind of grace, invisible yet undeniable as sound, that, however courted ("Lady Luck"), only sometimes visits. Theists of Luck tend to feel personally implicated by the results of games, to feel blessed or metaphysically afflicted, the recipient of some cosmic insult, convinced that some force field lavishes or withholds its powers without always letting Fortune's Fool know why. So Defoe's Robinson Crusoe describes his life as "Providence's chequer-work." However badly they're beaten, theists remain hopeful, since the very force that so evidently wrecked their ship tonight may choose to smile on their efforts to build another. Theists bet their birthday numbers on the Lotto, so if they hit they can confirm that they were born under a lucky star.

Atheists of Luck believe only in percentages, the ruthless rules of statistics, computer rollouts, and skill. To the atheist of luck, such as champion poker player Bobby Baldwin, "Luck is not really a factor, it's a myth." Sure, there are streaks—astonishing, gravity-defying ones. But this is only fitting in a random world where, however likely a thing is to happen, it need not happen. The atheist of Luck wouldn't have it any other way, and is willing to lay odds that, sooner or later, those Icarian sinners who fly against the laws of percentages will be brought back down to earth.

The more I reflect upon a great number of events, past or present, the more I recognize the effect of chance in all earthly things.

> TACITUS
> *Germanicus* (A.D. 99)

———•◆•———

In life we must make all due allowance for chance. Chance, in the last resort, is God.

> ANATOLE FRANCE
> *The Garden of Epicurus* (1926)
> translated by Alfred Allinson

———•◆•———

We can't suppress the fact that at one point everything and every law was decided according to the whims of chance—or luck—without reason entering the picture, except when the calculation of probabilities allowed it to.

> GEORGE BATAILLE
> *Guilty* (1961)
> translated by Bruce Boone

There are phenomenal runs of luck which defy any mathematical explanation—there are periods in which one cannot catch a hand, and periods in which one cannot *not* catch a hand, and that there *is* such a thing as absolute premonition of cards: the rock-bottom *surety* of what will happen next.

> DAVID MAMET
> "Things I Have Learned Playing Poker on the Hill" (1986)

———— •◆• ————

Luck! There is such a thing, and I know that there is, because it comes in two kinds. Good and bad.

> NICK "THE GREEK" DANDALOS
> quoted in Ted Thackrey Jr., *Gambling Secrets of Nick the Greek* (1968)

———— •◆• ————

When a guy finally gets his rushes in gambling nothing can stop him for a while.

> DAMON RUNYON
> "A Very Honorable Guy" (1929)

Once your luck starts to roll, there's not a damn thing you can do to stop it. It's like the whole world suddenly falls into place. You're kind of outside your body, and for the rest of the night you sit there watching yourself perform miracles. It doesn't really have anything to do with you anymore. It's out of your control, and as long as you don't think about it too much, you can't make a mistake.

> PAUL AUSTER
> *The Music of Chance* (1990)

———•◆•———

"When a man gets a streak of luck . . . he don't get tired. The luck gives in first. Luck," continued the gambler reflectively, "is a mighty queer thing. All you know about if for certain is that it's bound to change. And it's finding out when it's going to change that makes you."

> BRET HARTE
> "The Outcasts of Poker Flat" (1870)

———•◆•———

A dose of good luck will generally be followed by a stronger dose of bad.

> ANTHONY HOLDEN
> *Big Deal* (1990)

No matter what our character, no matter what our behavior, no matter if we are ugly, unkind, murderers, saints, guilty sinners, foolish, or wise, *we can get lucky.*

> MARIO PUZO
> *Inside Las Vegas* (1976)

———◆———

Dice will run the contrary way,
As well is known to all who play
And cards will conspire as in treason.

> THOMAS HOOD
> "Miss Kilmansegg and Her Precious Leg" (1841)

———◆———

Luck never made a man wise.

> SENECA
> *Letters to Lucilius* (first century)

———◆———

At gambling, the deadly sin is to mistake bad play for bad luck.

> IAN FLEMING
> *Casino Royale* (1953)

His luck went so bad, that when he caught the ace of spades it had a funeral parlor logo on it.

> TEX SHEAHAN
> quoted in Bobby Baldwin, *Tales Out of Tulsa* (1984)

Probability is the very guide of life.

> CICERO (106–43 B.C.)

Chance is perhaps the pseudonym of God when he did not want to sign.

> ANATOLE FRANCE
> *The Garden of Epicurus* (1926)
> translated by Alfred Allinson

Percentages are sticklers for the truth.

> NICK "THE GREEK" DANDALOS
> quoted in Cy Rice, *Nick the Greek: King of Gamblers* (1969)

The difference between your one- or two-tenths of a percent, and my five-tenths of a percent is just a matter of time.

> JOHN GOLLEHON
> *A Gambler's Bedside Reader* (1998)

Blasphemed his gods, the dice, and damned his fate.

ALEXANDER POPE
"Dunciad" (1728)

———•◆•———

In these matters luck seems to play a very great role, so that some meet with unexpected success while others fail in what they might expect . . . For it is agreed by all that one man may be more fortunate than another or even than himself at another time of life, not only in games but also in business, and with one man more than another and on one day more than another.

GEROLAMO CARDANO
The Book on Games of Chance (c. 1520)

———•◆•———

He went about with a sort of stealth, seeking inwardly for luck.

D. H. LAWRENCE
"The Rocking-Horse Winner" (1926)

———•◆•———

Don't worry, your luck will change; it'll get worse!

POPULAR SAYING

Sensible people don't expect justice from chance.

ALAN WYKES
The Complete Illustrated Guide to Gambling (1964)

———◆———

Play is a hand-to-hand encounter with Fate.

ANATOLE FRANCE
The Garden of Epicurus (1926)
translated by Alfred Allinson

———◆———

Chance fights ever on the side of the prudent.

EURIPIDES (480–406 B.C.)
Pirithous

———◆———

Almost all life depends on probabilities.

FRANÇOIS VOLTAIRE
Essays: Probabilities (1756)

———◆———

Care and diligence bring good luck.

THOMAS FULLER
Gnomologia (1732)

Moses took a chance.

AMERICAN PROVERB

———— • ◆ • ————

This is where I should have quit, but some kind of strange
sensation built up in me, a kind of challenge to fate, a kind of
desire to give it a flick on the nose, or stick my tongue at it.

FYODOR DOSTOEVSKY
The Gambler (1867)
translated by Victor Terras

Teach me to navigate the fjords of chance.

MALCOLM LOWRY
"The Pilgrim" (1962)

———— • ◆ • ————

The gambler seeks the gambling-house, and wonders, his
body all afire, shall I be lucky?

RIG VEDA

SOOTHSAYER: If thou dost play with him at any game
    Thou art sure to lose; and of that natural luck
    He beats thee 'gainst the odds.
ANTONY: The very dice obey him,
    And in our sports my better cunning faints
    Under his chance. If we draw lots he speeds,
    His cocks do win the battle still of mine
    When it is all to nought: and his quails ever
    Beat mine, inhoop'd, at odds.

WILLIAM SHAKESPEARE
Antony and Cleopatra (1607)

Handling the luck through adjustments in your play, is one of the great arts in gambling.

BOBBY BALDWIN
Tales Out of Tulsa (1984)

Luck is the art of being, or being is the art of welcoming and loving luck.

GEORGE BATAILLE
Guilty (1961)
translated by Bruce Boone

We do not what we ought;
What we ought not, we do;
And lean upon the thought
That chance will bring us through.

MATTHEW ARNOLD
"Empedocles on Etna" (1852)

———•◆•———

Fortune's a right whore:
If she gives aught, she deals it in small parcels,
That she may take away all at one sweep.

JOHN WEBSTER
The White Devil (1612)

———•◆•———

BENEATH THIS TREE
LIES THE BODY
OF
JOHN OAKHURST,
WHO STRUCK A STREAK OF BAD LUCK
ON THE 23rd of NOVEMBER, 1850,
AND
HANDED IN HIS CHECKS
ON THE 7TH DECEMBER, 1850.

BRET HARTE
"The Outcasts of Poker Flat" (1870)

Talent makes its own luck.

WILLIAM KENNEDY
Billy Phelan's Greatest Game (1978)

———◆———

Chance arises from disorder, not regularity. It demands randomness—its light sparkles in dark obscurity. We fail it when we shield it from misfortune, and its sparkle abandons it when failed.

GEORGE BATAILLE
Guilty (1961)
translated by Bruce Boone

———◆———

Chance favors only the prepared mind.

LOUIS PASTEUR
quoted in James H. Austin, *Chase, Chance, and Creativity*
(1977)

———◆———

We make our fortunes and call them fate.

BENJAMIN DISRAELI
quoted in James H. Austin, *Chase, Chance, and Creativity*
(1977)

His was that cold alert fury of the gambler who knows he may lose anyway but that with a second's flagging of the fierce constant will he is sure too: and who keeps suspense from ever crystallizing by sheer fierce manipulation of the cards or dice until the ducts and glands of luck begin to flow again.

WILLIAM FAULKNER
Absolom, Absolom (1936)

———— •◆• ————

People who deny that the laws of probability exist are generally very unintelligent. So although I have some skepticism, it's on a different level than the person on the street. Their skepticism is based on ignorance. Mine is based on philosophical bewilderment.

POKER PLAYER MIKE C.
quoted in David M. Hayano, *Poker Faces: The Life and Work of Professional Card Players* (1982)

———— •◆• ————

Luck cannot be shared, and to try to do so means risking its vanishing altogether.

JACK RICHARDSON
Memoir of a Gambler (1979)

No victor believes in chance.

> FRIEDRICH NIETZSCHE
> *Aphorisms* (1878)

———◆———

Bad luck or anguish sustains the possibility of luck.

> GEORGE BATAILLE
> *Guilty* (1961)
> translated by Bruce Boone

———◆———

"If I live long enough the luck will change. I have had bad luck now for fifteen years. If I ever get any good luck I will be rich." He grinned. "I am a really good gambler, really I would enjoy being rich."

"Do you have bad luck with all games?"

"With everything and with women." He smiled again, showing his bad teeth.

> ERNEST HEMINGWAY
> "The Gambler, the Nun, the Radio" (1933)

Chance is unintentional, it is capricious, but we needn't conclude that chance is immune from human intervention . . . In today's parlance, we have usually watered down *serendipity* to mean the good luck that comes solely by accident. We think of it as a result, not an ability. We have tended to lose sight of the element of sagacity.

> JAMES H. AUSTIN
> *Chase, Chance, and Creativity* (1977)

———— • ◆ • ————

"I'm cold," he explained, when the dice came by again, meaning the dice didn't yet feel right to his hand. He opened his collar, the place was so warm, and unbuttoned the pocket where the week's pay hid. When they came by again he felt a bit warmer. Bought two chips for a dollar and bet them both on the field. Saw the dice turn a five and watched the banker making two chips four.

> NELSON ALGREN
> "Stickman's Laughter" (1960)

When fortune calls, quick!—offer her a chair.

Luck can't be bought at the grocers.

If you have bread and butter, your luck is good.

Luck doesn't help those who won't cooperate.

Those who don't rely on luck lessen their bad luck.

To have bad luck, one must still have luck.

JEWISH PROVERBS

———•◆•———

He will win you,
By irresistible luck, within this fortnight
Enough to buy a barony.

BEN JONSON
"The Alchemist" (1612)

———•◆•———

Alea [chance] . . . tends rather to abolish natural or acquired individual differences, so that all can be placed on an absolutely equal footing to await the blind verdict of chance.

ROGER CAILLOIS
Man, Play, and Games (1979)

"Toward morning the farmer gets lucky," Frankie assured every farmer present. And the cards went around and around.

> NELSON ALGREN
> *The Man with the Golden Arm* (1949)

————•◆•————

Luck is always gonna break even. Everybody in the whole world is gonna get the same amount of luck.

> PUG PEARSON
> quoted in David Spanier, *Total Poker* (1977)

————•◆•————

Chance is the greatest novelist in the world.

> HONORÉ DE BALZAC (1799–1850)

————•◆•————

Love is a lottery.

> JULES MICHELET (1798–1874)

I'll tell you what luck is, so. It's a line in which one side is wrong and the other is right. Now most folks try to keep as close to that line as they can. To be on that line would be perfect and that's impossible. You keep on sliding back and forth across it. That line is what most people define as luck.

PUG PEARSON
quoted in Jon Bradshaw, *Fast Company* (1975)

Is there such a thing as luck? Yes. There is such a thing as luck. There is such a thing as a *run of luck*. This is an instructive insight I have gained from poker—that all things have a rhythm, even the most seemingly inanimate of statistics.

DAVID MAMET
"Things I Have Learned Playing Poker on the Hill" (1986)

If you should play roulette, put twenty-five francs on for me just for luck.

ANTON CHEKHOV
Letters (1891)
translated by Constance Garnett

5

The Juice

If all my bets were safe, there just wouldn't be any juice.

AXEL FREED
in James Toback (screenwriter)
The Gambler (1974)

Pool juice got nerves.

WALTER TEVIS
The Hustler (1959)

*He places the bet, juices flow, he really feels alive:
action. When the bet is on, his existence is confirmed.*

HENRY LESIEUR
The Chase

In Fyodor Dostoevsky's remarkable novel *The Gambler* (1867)—a work dictated in three weeks to pay off debts—the protagonist finally enjoys a spectacular win. Almost immediately he goes on a wild halfhearted spree as if to throw the money away as fast as he can. Winning is exhilarating but ultimately irrelevant to him, losing excruciating in the act but ultimately relevant only in that it puts him out of action: The juice is the thing.

Juice refers to the rush of sensations that happen inside the gambler, switching on the nervous system, activating its receptivity to a variety of sensations. The rush of juice is an intensely private experience, never truly observable from outside. In that sense it resists expression, as when one tries to describe the symptoms of one's cold, and is forced into clumsy overdramatic metaphors like freezing and burning.

The magic of Dostoevsky's novel is its conveyance of some of the lure and draw of gambling, and of the feverish intoxication it produces in a man who lives for action. In odd, disembodied moments of clarity he achieves the distance from gambling to recognize its (for him) inseparable absurdity and sublimity, yet the giddy vertiginous sensations of the act itself have become as necessary as oxygen; only action can encapsulate him in the charged air he needs; only action produces the flow of juice along his nerves that he requires like a transfusion.

"To be on the wire is life; the rest is waiting," the tightrope artist Karl Wallenda is reputed to have said on going back up on the wire after members of his troupe had met with a fatal accident. It is a sentiment that requires no explanation to those who gamble, who feel most alive under conditions of risk, and who love the sweet, sharp strains of edge music, in whatever key.

Here the nerves may stand on end and scream to themselves, but a tranquility as from heaven is only interrupted by the click of chips. The higher the stakes, the more quiet the scene.

STEPHEN CRANE
"A Game of Poker" (1899)

He felt something icy move up and down his spine as he took another sip of the coffee and brandy and put the cup down very slowly and deliberately, not too showy, but enough so Lancey could see it if he were looking for signs.

RICHARD JESSUP
The Cincinnati Kid (1963)

The fascination of danger is at the bottom of all great passions. There is no fullness of pleasure unless the precipice is near. It is the mingling of terror with delight that intoxicates. And what is more terrifying than play?

ANATOLE FRANCE
The Garden of Epicurus (1926)
translated by Alfred Allinson

The pure sensuality of the betting moment . . . It is a neurological jolt made up of greed, lust and excitement mixed together with a strong dose of fear.

EDWARD ALLEN
"Penny Ante" (1992)

———————◆———————

Serious action is a serious ride, and rides of this kind are all but arranged out of everyday life.

IRVING GOFFMAN
Where the Action Is (1967)

———————◆———————

To dare, to take risks, to bear uncertainty, to endure tension— these are the essence of the play spirit. Tension adds to the importance of the game and, as it increases, enables the player to forget he is playing.

JOHAN HUIZINGA
Homo Ludens (1949)

The ebb and flow of opposite movements—the shocks of alternate hope and fear, infinitely varied in the countenance, not only of the actors, but also of the spectators. What is visible, however, is nothing in comparison to the secret agony.

> ANDREW STEINMETZ
> *The Gaming Table* (1870)

———◆———

I learned more intimately than ever that there's a relationship between heartbeat and pleasure, heartbeat and fear.

> STEPHEN DUNN
> "Gambling: Remembrances and Assertions" (1993)

———◆———

I'd wager he lost at least five pounds through perspiration every dice game.

> NICK "THE GREEK" DANDALOS
> on "Diamond" Jim Brady
> quoted in Cy Rice, *Nick the Greek: King of Gamblers* (1969)

———◆———

"It's ruthless. Completely ruthless. The cards terrorize you. Seconds stretch. It's like having the worst flu you can imagine for twenty seconds."

> FREDERICK BARTHELME
> *Bob the Gambler* (1997)

The pursuit of vertigo . . . an attempt to momentarily destroy the stability of perception and inflict a kind of voluptuous panic upon an otherwise lucid mind. In all cases, it is a question of surrendering to a kind of spasm, seizure, or shock which destroys reality with sovereign brusqueness.

> ROGER CAILLOIS
> *Man, Play, and Games* (1979)

I can't tell you how thrilling the game is . . . If I had money to spare I believe I should spend the whole year gambling and walking about the magnificent halls of the casino.

> ANTON CHEKHOV
> letter to his sister (1891)
> translated by Constance Garnett

Gamblers are as happy as most people, being always *excited*. Women, wine, fame, the table, even Ambition, *sate* now and then; but every turn of the card, and cast of the dice, keeps the Gamester alive: besides one can Game ten times longer than one can do anything else.

> GEORGE GORDON, LORD BYRON
> "Detached Thoughts" (1821)

In a large-bet, well-made match . . . the mob scene quality, the sense that sheer chaos is about to break loose . . . is quite strong, an effect which is only heightened by the intense stillness that falls with instant suddenness, rather as if someone had turned off the current, when the slit gong sounds, the cocks are put down, and battle begins.

CLIFFORD GEERTZ
"Deep Play: Notes on the Balinese Cockfight" (1972)

———•◆•———

[Gambling] heats the mind like an oven.

HENRY WARD BEECHER
Gamblers and Gambling (1896)

———•◆•———

Gambling makes the mind burn. Can this be turned into the fire of purification and understanding?

MIRON STABINSKY WITH JEREMY SILMAN
Zen and the Art of Casino Gambling (1995)

———•◆•———

Such relief when my face card came—like my head was cracking open.

FREDERICK BARTHELME
Bob the Gambler (1997)

Prew felt a salve of relief grease over him for sure now he knew Warden had no trips.

JAMES JONES
From Here to Eternity (1951)

———•◆•———

The game, like an endlessly circling bird, moved with a slow inexorable pace toward the center pot of money that grew magically with each dealt hand; revolving hands of cards, accompanied by a musical comment of silver upon silver tossed into the center of the table as the chant was heard, so soft as to be a litany calling on ghostly assistance and deliverance.

RICHARD JESSUP
The Cincinnati Kid (1963)

———•◆•———

It's an excited, anxious state, but my nature sometimes begs for that.

FYODOR DOSTOEVSKY
letter to Anna Grigoryevna (May 21, 1867)
Complete Letters (1988)
translated by David A. Lowe

In games of pure chance the tension felt by the player is only feebly communicated to the onlooker.

> JOHAN HUIZINGA
> *Homo Ludens* (1949)

———◆———

"Zero!" the croupier announced.

"Wow!!!" Grandmother turned to me in a frenzy of triumph.

I was myself a gambler; I felt it that very moment. My limbs were trembling, and I felt dazed.

> FYODOR DOSTOEVSKY
> *The Gambler* (1867)
> translated by Victor Terras

———◆———

The most common Tell is the pulse in a man's neck. On a lot of people, the pulse in the neck is visible. If so, a man can't hide it, since nobody can control their heartbeat in stress situations. When you see a man's neck just throbbing away, you know he's excited, and usually he's excited because he is bluffing.

> DOYLE BRUNSON
> *How I Made $1,000,000 Playing Poker* (1979)

Now all my senses were opened: I could hear every sound in the casino, discern every face that was watching the play at the table.

> JACK RICHARDSON
> *Memoir of a Gambler* (1979)

———◆———

His hands become nervous when he picks up the cards, exactly as if he were holding live birds instead of inanimate pieces of cardboard.

> MAXIM GORKY (1868–1936)
> describing Leo Tolstoy at cards

———◆———

Almost all gamesters learn to control their faces . . . The Hand blabs secrets shamelessly.

> STEPHAN ZWEIG
> *Four-and-Twenty Hours in a Woman's Life* (1926)
> translated by Eden and Cedar Paul

I was suddenly back in my own skin, the numbness had peeled off, but I felt calm. If my luck was so bad I couldn't throw one pass on the up-and-up, then I deserved to lose, it was my proper *bachi* . . . I [could] only lay low and not take any chances and wait for the bad luck to pass.

I threw down the 200 in my left hand. "Here's 200 more. All or nothing."

MILTON MURAYAMA
All I Ask for Is My Body (1975)

Two handsome men are absorbed in a game of backgammon. Though they have been playing all day, they still do not seem tired and order a servant to light the lamp on a short stand. One of the players holds the dice in his hand and, before finally placing them in the box, prays earnestly for a good throw.

SEI SHŌNAGON
"Two Handsome Men"
The Pillow Book of Sei Shōnagon

That specific disease in which the suspension of the whole nervous system on a chance or risk becomes as necessary as the dram to the drunkard.

GEORGE ELIOT
Middlemarch (1872)

———◆———

Without heeding the ringing in my ears or the quickened beat of my heart, I took out two twenty-franc pieces—I can see them to this day! The dates on them were worn off and Napoleon, stamped in effigy, seemed to grimace. Replacing the purse in my pocket, I approached a card-table clasping the two coins in my damp palm.

HONORÉ DE BALZAC
The Wild Ass's Skin (1831)

———◆———

There is something special about that feeling which you have, all alone, in a foreign country, far from home and from your friends, now knowing what you'll eat tomorrow, as you bet your last, your very, very last gulden.

FYODOR DOSTOEVSKY
The Gambler (1867)
translated by Victor Terras

I have seen a pregnant woman stand at a 21 game, oblivious to labor pains, until we thought we were going to become midwives, and leave only when we summoned an ambulance.

HAROLD S. SMITH SR. WITH JOHN WESLEY NOBLE
I Want to Quit Winners (1961)

———•◆•———

What is it that makes the placing of a bet and the awaiting of its outcome so very exciting to most of us? It isn't easy to answer these questions. You won't find the answer by trying to observe your own reactions to the turning wheel at Monte Carlo; you'll be too busy observing the *wheel*.

ALAN WYKES
The Complete Illustrated Guide to Gambling (1964)

———•◆•———

This was the first time he had seriously confronted what he was doing, and the force of that awareness came very abruptly— with a surging of his pulse and a frantic pounding in his head. He was about to gamble his life on that table, he realized, and the insanity of that risk filled him with a kind of awe.

PAUL AUSTER
The Music of Chance (1990)

Billy sat with his arms folded. Keeping cool. But folks, he was really feeling the sweet pressure, and had been, all through the hand: rising, rising. And he keeps winning on top of that. It was so great he was almost ready to cream . . . He ran his fingers over the table's green felt, fingered his pile of quarters, flipped through his stack of bills while he waited for the Lemon squash. Goddamn, it's good.

> WILLIAM KENNEDY
> *Billy Phelan's Greatest Game* (1978)

If I lose today, I can look forward to winning tomorrow, and if I win today, I can expect to lose tomorrow. A sure thing is no fun.

> CHICO MARX
> quoted in Joe Adamson, *Groucho, Harpo, Chico, and Sometimes Zeppo* (1973)

If I've got action, anything is possible. If I haven't got action, nothing is possible.

> SAL THE DICE MAN
> quoted in David Spanier, *Easy Money: Inside the Gambler's Mind* (1987)

6

Winning

As I walk along the Bois Bou-long
With an independent air.
You can hear the girls declare:
"He must be a millionaire,"
You can hear them sigh
And wish to die,
You can see them wink the other eye
At the man who broke the bank at Monte Carlo

> FRED GILBERT (1850–1903)
> "The Man Who Broke the Bank at Monte Carlo"

I feel like I done when Slippery Sun
Romped 'ome a winner at 30 to 1
Somebody's singing inside me.

> ALAN PATRICK HERBERT
> *Derby Day* (1932)

There are times when you surf on chance, riding and gliding inside it, swept along by and just ahead of its force, and you can do no wrong. The big hands swell like they'll never crest, and you're encapsulated in a blessed pocket, others wiping out all around, but not you.

For the delirious duration of these streaks you seem to catch every card, make every hand, communicate directly with the gambling gods, bask in a dice-rolling zone. Every gambler has had such moments of invincibility, and once you've had them you want them again. There's nothing like the high of winning. You get so much. Your inward prayers answered, as if your imagination itself drove a particular horse under the wire, or caused a ball to find its proper groove.

And at the end you have more money than you started with.

But winning would have little of its exhilaration without an intimate acquaintance with losing. I have no evidence that Emily Dickinson was a gambler, but the Belle of Amherst nailed this relation between winning and losing when she wrote:

> For each ecstatic instant
> We must an anguish pay
> In keen and quivering ratio
> To the ecstasy.

The highs of gambling are paid for by the lows, made possible by them. Sure, there are a few people who always seem to win at games of chance, like James Bond. But how much do they enjoy gambling? The joy of occasionally winning for most of us mortals comes from the thrill of risk and proximity to the precipice. The fact that we often fall makes so much more special those lovely floating moments when the tightrope across the chasm of losing feels miraculously wide and secure.

Winning can also be an unexpectedly shared experience. Among the joys of gambling are the sudden bonds that form around a group bet in a bar or a hot shooter at a craps table. As gambling expert Darwin Ortiz describes it, "Craps players at the table often develop such an 'us versus them' mentality that it almost seems like a team sport. When the table is really hot and everyone is winning, it's a communal experience." At such times the group ignores the nay-sayers, or those whom Larry Merchant refers to as "Judases who bet with the house." In a gentler expression of this, Clifford Geertz describes how, among Balinese cockfighters, "there is a special word for betting against the grain, which is also the word for 'pardon me.'"

In play there are two pleasures for your choosing—The one is winning, and the other losing.

>   GEORGE GORDON, LORD BYRON
>   *Don Juan* (1826)

I've got magic powers. I'm scorching. I'm hot as a pistol.

>   AXEL FREED
>   to his bookie
>   in James Toback (screenwriter)
>   *The Gambler* (1974)

"Lord, what a day! Them cards were so good to me today!"

>   ROBERT ABEL
>   "One Up" (1991)

I want it to be slow so I can roll every minute of winning around in my mouth half-a-dozen times.

>   JACK RICHARDSON
>   *Xmas in Las Vegas* (1962)

If you win, and you're not excited, then you haven't won at all.

> JOHN GOLLEHON
> *A Gambler's Little Instruction Book* (1994)

———◆———

He returned, with doleful face, as usual, saying things had gone badly, that though he had not lost, he had not won more than one hundred and fifty gulden! One hundred and fifty gulden—one's brain reels at the thought of such a sum.

> ANNA DOSTOEVSKY
> *The Diary of Dostoevsky's Wife* (August 20, 1867)
> translated by Marge Pemberton (1928)

———◆———

When I won, I felt as if a constellation in my image should appear in the morning sky.

> JACK RICHARDSON
> *Memoir of a Gambler* (1979)

What non-gamblers do not know is the feeling of *virtue* . . . when the dice roll as one commands. And that omniscient goodness when the card you need rises to the top of the deck to greet your delighted yet confident eyes. It is as close as I have ever come in my life to a religious feeling.

MARIO PUZO
Inside Las Vegas (1976)

Playing a winning rush usually gives momentum to all of the elements of winning play.

BOBBY BALDWIN
Tales Out of Tulsa (1984)

The Stickman at the crap table should be a Mary Poppins optimist, delight in his voice when he calls out a winner.

MARIO PUZO
Inside Las Vegas (1976)

Sometimes a race unfolds exactly as you've envisioned it, with the horses cleaving to a pattern in your brain.

BILL BARICH
Laughing in the Hills (1980)

I have seen many poor winners. Most are eventually brought back to reality. The game itself will reveal to them that they are the victim of an essential error: they have attributed their success to divine intervention.

DAVID MAMET
"Things I Have Learned Playing Poker on the Hill" (1986)

I'll give you revenge another time, when you are not so indifferent; you are thinking of something else now, and play too negligently; the coldness of a losing gamester lessens the pleasure of the winner. I'd no more play with a man that slighted his ill fortune, than I'd make love to a woman who undervalued the loss of her reputation.

WILLIAM CONGREVE
The Way of the World (1700)

"Slots giveth and slots taketh away," I said.

"They're good when they come in, aren't they? Nothing like that sound. Nothing."

FRED BARTHELME
Bob the Gambler (1997)

The table was bulging with players while a crowd formed from nowhere. I swear, people must have come in off the street. It was as if someone changed the Dune's famous sign from: "All-You-Can-Eat Buffet after 4 PM" to: ALL-YOU-CAN-WIN CRAPS TABLE GOING ON RIGHT NOW.

> JOHN GOLLEHON
> *A Gambler's Bedside Reader* (1998)

I won so much gelt off Smart Henry it looked like I was smuggling coconuts in my pockets.

> MINNESOTA FATS WITH TOM FOX
> *The Great Bank Shot and Other Great Robberies* (1966)

To be a winner, you have to really want to be a winner.

> AVERY CARDOZA
> *How to Play Winning Poker* (1987)

"Just breaking even" is the habitual language of a winner disguising for one reason or another his success.

> DAVID SPANIER
> *Total Poker* (1977)

Beware, above all, of the man who simply tells you he broke even. *He* is the big winner.

> ANTHONY HOLDEN
> *Big Deal* (1990)

———————•◆•———————

The pain of losing is diverting. So is the thrill of winning. Winning, however, is lonelier, as those you've won money from are not likely to commiserate with you. Winning takes getting used to.

> DAVID MAMET
> "Things I Have Learned Playing Poker on the Hill" (1986)

———————•◆•———————

We lose—because we win—
Gamblers—recollecting which—
Toss their dice again.

> EMILY DICKINSON (1830–86)

He is either lifted up to the top of mad joy with success, or plung'd to the bottom of despair by misfortune, always in extreams, always in a storm; this minute the gamester's countenance is so serene and calm, and one would think nothing could disturb it, and the next minute so stormy and tempestuous that it threatens destruction to itself and others.

CHARLES COTTON
The Compleate Gamester (1674)

Winning and losing and the expectations therefrom are diverting. I conceive there would be no pleasure properly so called if a man were sure to win. It is the reconciling of uncertainty to our desires that creates the satisfaction.

FREDERICK BRANDT
Games, Gaming and Gamesters' Law

Nobody is *always* a winner, and anybody who says he is, is either a liar or doesn't play poker.

AMARILLO SLIM
quoted in David Spanier, *Total Poker* (1977)

Sometimes when you win, you really lose. Sometimes when you lose, you really win. Sometimes when you tie, you actually win *or* lose, and sometimes when you win or lose, you *actually* tie . . . Winning and losing is all one big globule from which one extracts what one needs.

> GLORIA
> in Ron Shelton (screenwriter)
> *White Men Can't Jump* (1991)

———— ◆ ————

There are many victories that are worse than a defeat.

> GEORGE ELIOT (1819–80)

———— ◆ ————

If there's no risk in losing, there's no high in winning. I have only a limited amount of time on this earth, and I want to live every second of it. That's why I'm willing to play anyone in the world for any amount.

> JACK STRAUSS
> quoted in Alvin Alvarez, *The Biggest Game in Town* (1983)

———— ◆ ————

Hell, for a gambler, is a game he can't lose.

> PAT JORDAN
> "Watching Dad Gamble" (1993)

It is a fine thing to get a peck or a bushel of gold just by betting for it, but the tremulous rapture of mingled hope and fear is almost compensation enough even if one loses. Next to the pleasure of winning is the pleasure of losing; only stagnation is unendurable.

> HUBERT HOWE BANCROFT
> *California Inter Pocula* (1882)

To love the game itself is a fine thing; it is loving the art you live by. There are many things to love in the art—the excitement of it, the difficulty, the use of skill—but . . . to play pool you had to want to win and to want this without excuses and without self-deception. Only then did you have the right to love the game itself.

> WALTER TEVIS
> *The Hustler* (1959)

AXEL: I'm blessed. Double it.
DEALER: You want to double on 18 sir?
AXEL: Yes. Give me the three.

> AXEL FREED
> in James Toback (screenwriter)
> *The Gambler* (1974)

There was nothing in life like this. Nothing. To stroke and hit the cue ball, to watch the colored ball roll with the certitude that he himself imposed on it, to see and hear the colored ball fall into the pocket he had chosen, was exquisite.

WALTER TEVIS
The Color of Money (1984)

———— • ◆ • ————

When he called the seventh number and explained dramatically that whoever had punched five numbers in a row had won the jackpot of fifty-five dollars, she listened in smiling disbelief that there was that much money in his pocket. It was then that the woman beside her leaned toward her and said excitedly, "Look, lady, you got it!"

DOROTHY WEST
"Jack in the Pot"

As they passed the last of the crap tables, a very old man was shaking the dice fervidly; now, with a broad, sweeping movement he threw them powerfully from the side of his hand out onto the long green . . . The number that came up was eleven. *"Natural!"* cried the old man joyfully, leaning forward to pull in a pile of bills.

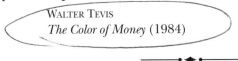

WALTER TEVIS
The Color of Money (1984)

The next best thing to playing and winning is playing and losing. The main thing is to play.

NICK "THE GREEK" DANDOLOS
quoted in Ted Thackrey Jr., *Gambling Secrets of Nick the Greek* (1968)

7

Losing

Games in which all may win, such games remain as yet in this world uninvented.

> HERMAN MELVILLE
> *The Confidence-Man* (1857)

Losing's easier than winning. Am I right or not?

> MONKEY
> in James Toback (screenwriter)
> *The Gambler* (1974)

Tapioca time . . . Busted. El Broko!

> JOSEPH WALSH (SCREENWRITER)
> *California Split* (1973)

Single O, tap city, Hocus brokus . . . the variety and humorous dolefulness of the expressions gamblers use to describe being flat busted suggests a familiarity and even a laughing pact with losing. To say "I'm tapped" is to say to a fellow gambler, "I had action," and more often than not to receive a knowing if not a consoling nod.

For a variety of reasons, losing is a purer feeling than winning. (For one thing, it's harder to know what to do with a win, especially around the pigeons you've just finished plucking.) While winning is intimately connected to and takes meaning from the possibility of losing, losing is all too sufficient to itself, and can be a far more intense experience, whether one faces it with external stoicism or speaks a body English of jerks and twitches.

Losing what you shouldn't—going "on tilt" with money you can't afford to lose, disastrous streaks where you feel personally singled out and cursed—can be a private hell all the hotter since one is stoking one's own fire and could (hypothetically) step out of it at any moment. This kind of losing can burn itself into the brain, or, worse, build up so much scar tissue that it affects the ability to feel at all. One becomes poor company.

Yet there is often, even in one's stuckest moments, something compelling about the vertiginous downward ride of losing. For psychologists, like one Sigmund Freud, this is because gambling is in complex ways about self-sabotage (as well as other ways of flogging oneself that I'd blush to mention), a love of losing. To this the novelist and lifelong gambler William Saroyan is supposed to have said, leaping onto a coldhearted craps table, "I don't care what Freud says, I want to win!"

When it comes to pyschoanalytic discussions of gambling, especially by nongamblers, I am tempted toward Mario Puzo's blunt assessement:

> Nearly everything I have ever read or just been told about why people gamble is just plain bullshit. Some psychiatrists claim gambling is masochistic, that gamblers want to lose to punish themselves. Sure some do. Some people like to jump off the Empire State Building. But millions go up to look at the view.

Puzo's point about every gambler's relation to gambling being different seems a necessary one. And yet, too, I must admit a general sense in which, as Stephen Dunn writes, the typical recreational gambler accepts losing "because it has interesting neighbors." The megadealer like Donald Trump is proud to say, "A gambler is someone who plays slot machines. I prefer to own slot machines." Or, as one casino owner says to another: "It's the risk I like about owning a casino. Some days you win, other days you win more."

I suspect your average gamblers are proud to say the opposite, and willing to get taken for a ride because they enjoy its hopes and fears, and that this accounts for much of the fraternity of feelings among us suckers being bused to Atlantic City: We the people don't in the end mind playing against the House percentage—the rake is a kind of seat rental at Life's table. We don't mind not sitting on a pile of portfolios as long as we can get a ride for our money. Sure, the Trumps of the world may grind us down in their Monopoly game, take a piece of us when we land on Boardwalk or Park Place, and the odds are that we'll lose more than we win. But if you're not holding trumps, the role of the hopeful underdog on the bus, the flutter of excitement onboard the Express as the bus banks toward glittering lights, is not a wholly unenviable one.

My hands were shaking, my thoughts confused, and even when losing, I was somehow almost glad, I kept saying, "Let it be, let it be!"

> FYODOR DOSTOEVSKY
> letter to Anna (May 21, 1867)
> *Complete Letters*
> translated by David A. Lowe

———◆———

No use gambling if you can't lose your head once in awhile.

> LARRY MERCHANT
> *The National Football Lottery* (1973)

———◆———

So the gambler, lest he should lose, does not stop losing.

> OVID (43 B.C.–A.D. 18)
> *Ars Amat*

———◆———

To lose filled me with such black feelings that only the sternest mental efforts could drag me back to the point where I could admit that a single loss had not turned me into one of gambling's lepers.

> JACK RICHARDSON
> *Memoir of a Gambler* (1979)

He was so sure he would lose that he had not played everything—
as if to prolong the sensation of losing.

ANDRÉ MALRAUX
Man's Fate (1934)

———•◆•———

They gambled with me for my heart with all kinds of games.
They defeated me and took it away.

AS-SANAWBARI
quoted in in Franz Rosenthal, *Gambling in Islam* (1975)

———•◆•———

The eternal poker pessimist, like the compulsive gambler,
wants to lose. Losing makes him happy, confirming as it does
a wide range of his most deeply held beliefs: that life is a
bum rap, that his true qualities will never be appreciated by
a cruely misguided world, that he is generally undervalued
and misunderstood. He will go on cheerfully defying the
odds under the endearing delusion that there is more to
him than meets the eye.

ANTHONY HOLDEN
Big Deal (1990)

The solemn resolutions, which are nevertheless broken, never to do it again, the stupefying pleasure and the bad conscience which tells the subject he is ruining himself.

SIGMUND FREUD
"Dostoevsky and Parricide" (1928)

———— • ◆ • ————

I have been in Wiesbaden five days already and have lost everything, including my watch and I am even in debt at the hotel.

FYODOR DOSTOEVSKY
letter to Ivan Turgenev (March 15, 1865)
Complete Letters
translated by David A. Lowe

It's a terrible feeling to be far ahead and then start losing in a way that you just can't stop . . . There comes a point when you begin to think you know the cards before they're dealt. You've made a big bet, you're holding an eighteen and the dealer is showing an eight, and you think you've "pushed," you're safe. Then you think, Unless she has an ace. No sooner have you had the second thought than you know that she has an ace. . . . And when she flips her down card there it is, the ace. And you lose again. Then you think that you caused her to have the ace by thinking it.

FREDRICK AND STEVEN BARTHLEME
"Good Losers" (1999)

Bad beats haunt you like bad dreams.

ALVIN ALVAREZ
"No Limit" (1994)

Now it seemed that my pain had no antecedents, no history in common with anything produced by past imagination. For the thousandth time in my life I learned that there were no fixed categories of distress for the healthy ego.

JACK RICHARDSON
Memoir of a Gambler (1979)

I like the uncertainty of it. I like the threat of losing. I mean the idea that I could lose but that somehow I won't, because I don't want to. That's what I like. I love winning, even though it never lasts.

AXEL FREED
in James Toback (screenwriter)
The Gambler (1974)

———— •◆• ————

Who among us has not sympathized with chessmaster Aron Nimzovitch (1886–1935), who jumped on a table during a tournament and shouted, "Why must I lose to this idiot?" If it happens too often, losing leads to self-loathing, despair, and frightening eruptions of bile. I've heard of extreme cases where players got so sick and tired of losing at pool that they sank to bowling.

ROBERT BYRNE
Byrne's Wonderful World of Pool and Billiards (1996)

———— •◆• ————

Big egos and big losses go hand in hand.

JOHN GOLLEHON
A Gambler's Little Instruction Book (1994)

Winners tell funny stories, and losers yell, "Deal, dealer, deal!"

POKER SAYING

Show me a gambler and I'll show you a loser.

MARIO PUZO
Fools Die (1978)

To gamble is to risk, to approach the "ruin factor." When I was poor the ruin factor was not important. Hell, I was ruined anyway.

MARIO PUZO
Inside Las Vegas (1976)

July 19, 1867

Soon he was back again, having lost everything, including his wedding ring that he had pawned on the way for 20 francs.

July 23, 1867

Of course he lost, and came back to ask my last thaler from me, though it was all we had left. I implored him not to touch it as fate obviously didn't mean us to win. He admitted my point, but took the money and lost it.

> ANNA DOSTOEVSKY
> *The Diary of Dostoevsky's Wife*
> translated by Marge Pemberton (1928)

I play in order to lose. That's what gets my juice going. If I only bet on the games I know, I could at least break even.

> AXEL FREED
> in James Toback (screenwriter)
> *The Gambler* (1974)

He was all red and in a sweat though the room was not hot. And his face was painful and piteous to see, particularly from its helpless efforts to seem calm.

> ROSTOV LOSING HIS FORTUNE
> in Leo Tolstoy
> *War and Peace* (1869)

Anything with the name of loss attached to it sliced the old man's heart into sections.

STEPHEN CRANE
"A Game of Poker" (1899)

⸺◆⸺

The pile grew again. And grew a little more. Until, all of a sudden, it was the smallest pile he had ever seen and everyone was smiling, because it wasn't there at all.

NELSON ALGREN
"Stickman's Laughter" (1960)

⸺◆⸺

I felt shitty about the money we'd lost, but I thought we might win it back, sooner or later. I was tired of trying to understand the attraction—Jewel said it was like drugs, the same thing, but I wasn't sure. There were many pleasures, and it didn't seem to matter that much whether you won or lost. I sort of felt it was more exhilarating to lose a lot than win a little. Losing meant you had to play more, try harder. Losing burned intensely; winning became tepid fast.

FREDRICK BARTHELME
Bob the Gambler (1997)

A losing gambler is an albatross to everyone around him. He doesn't get those warm glowing smiles from his family. In a crap game he leaves the dice so damp with defeat that the stick man pushes them clinically to one side as though they were infected.

JACK RICHARDSON
Xmas in Las Vegas (1962)

———◆———

He joked less the more he lost. . . . The two men became so obsessed with their game that they began to accuse one another of cheating. Their fists waved threateningly over the draughtboard. Their voices became heated . . . Dad, losing steadily, abused his opponents virulently; his opponent replied with incredible vehemence. I got worried. Dad placed an absurd bet on himself and his opponent doubled it.

BEN OKRI
The Famished Road (1991)

"I bet you had fun, losing your head. It's always nice to feel the risks fall off your back. And winning; that can be heavy on your back too, like a monkey. You drop that load too when you find an excuse. Then, afterward, all you got to do is learn to feel sorry for yourself . . . A sport enjoyed by all. Especially the born losers."

BERT TO FAST EDDIE
in Walter Tevis
The Hustler (1959)

———•◆•———

Losing as much money as I can get hold of is an instant solution to my economic problems.

LUCIAN FREUD (b. 1922)

———•◆•———

The games became burning lights on the floor of my withdrawal, and later, while I slept, there were poker chips falling through my dreams.

JIM LEWIS
Real Gone (1993)

My only worry about my husband's gambling is that he may lose.

SPANISH PROVERB

I worry about compulsive gamblers but I don't know what to do about it. They don't come into the casino wearing scarlet letters.

JIMMY PARRY, CASINO CEO
quoted in Timothy L. O'Brien, *Bad Bet* (1998)

A gentleman, whom ill fortune had hurried into passion, took a box of dice to a side-table, and there fell to throwing by himself; at length swears with an emphasis; "Damme, now I throw for nothing, I can win a thousand pounds; but when I play for money, I lose my arse."

NICHOLAS LEATHERMORE
The Nicker Nicked: or, The Cheats of Gambling Discovered

They would be sitting there for hours, keeping track of what number came up, and marking it down. They might not make a bet in an hour. They seemed to have it timed perfectly, just when to lose. A fellow there told me they were playing a system, and they only bet at certain times. When I bet without a system, why, they looked at me like I was crazy. I don't know why, because I was losing just as good as they were.

WILL ROGERS
"A Visit to Monte Carlo"
A Will Rogers Treasury (1982)

———— ◆ ————

It seemed to me that calculating your chances really means rather little, and certainly isn't as important as some gamblers make it out to be. They sit there with sheets of graph paper before them, mark every stroke, reckon, compute the odds, calculate, and finally place their bets. They lose, exactly as we simple mortals who play without calculating anything.

FYODOR DOSTOEVSKY
The Gambler (1867)
translated by Victor Terras

Well, to make a fair bankroll short, it don't take me long to learn about the game.

WILL ROGERS
"A Visit to Monte Carlo"
A Will Rogers Treasury (1982)

———————•◆•———————

You see people getting 20,000 to 30,000 franks daily. (You don't see losers.) What makes them sacred? I need the money more than they do. I took a further risk and lost. I began losing the last of my money, getting feverishly irritated, and lost. I started pawning my clothing. Anna Grigorievna pawned everything of hers, her last things.

FYODOR DOSTOEVSKY
letter to Apollon Maykov (August 28, 1867)
Complete Letters
translated by David A. Lowe

I hit an unlucky streak, and we had to move to less expensive quarters. Things went from bad to worse, and I found myself telling her night after night the same old story—"The sucker drew out." I came home one night and she wasn't there, and also missing were her clothes and suitcases. All I found was a big printed note on the table. It said: "Gone with the sucker."

POKER PLAYER
quoted in Allen Dowling
The Great American Pastime (1970)

———— •◆• ————

I played . . . with such bad luck that I was soon left without a sequin. I was obliged to tell [the lady] of my losses, and it was at her request that I sold all her diamonds, losing what I got for them . . . I still gamed, but for small stakes, waiting for the slow return of good luck.

GIACOMO JACOPO CASANOVA DE SEINGALT (1725–98)
Memoirs
translated by Arthur Machen

Losers exaggerate. That's because they're not trying to convey *what really happened* so much as *how bad they feel*. You shouldn't challenge their outrageous claims of misfortune. Merely do your duty as a human being and commiserate.

MIKE CARO
Mike Caro on Gambling (1984)

———•◆•———

He would yell, suddenly, "Fade me," and then he'd roll the dice—anywhere, even on the taut blanket of an army cot! Real quick. For a while he was lucky, but his luck reversed soon and he couldn't make a single point. He was always looking for a backer. "The arm's gold," he'd say, "Can't miss because it's gold." Then when he'd lose he'd cuss like hell.

NELSON ALGREN
on the source for *Man with the Golden Arm*
quoted in H. E. F. Donohue
Conversations with Nelson Algren (1964)

They are not shaking or sweating, but they create a tension thick with guilt and persecution. Their luck being inversely proportionate to their need, they always lose. Sera is disturbed when they appear, and turns away, not from the hopelessness of their situation, which they take far too seriously, but from the intensity of their suffering, which will forever make them victims in their own mind.

JOHN O'BRIEN
Leaving Las Vegas (1990)

———•◆•———

"I think we should start over," Mrs. Hutchinson said, as quietly as she could. "I tell you it wasn't *fair.* You didn't give him enough time to choose. *Every*body saw that."

SHIRLEY JACKSON
The Lottery (1949)

At Bayonne, in 1725, a French officer, in a rage at billiards, jammed a billiard-ball in his mouth, where it stuck fast, arresting respiration, until it was, with difficulty, extracted by a surgeon . . . It is well known that gamblers . . . have eaten up the cards, crushed up the dice, broken the tables, damaged the furniture, and finally "pitched into" each other . . . A mad player at Naples bit the table with such violence that his teeth went deep into the wood.

ANDREW STEINMETZ
The Gaming Table (1870)

In the end, with loud protestations that he could lose like a gentleman, the cook's last money was staked on the game and lost. Whereupon he leaned his head on his hands and wept. Wolf Larsen looked curiously at him.

"Hump," he said to me, elaborately polite, "kindly take Mr. Mugridge's arm and help him on deck. He is not feeling very well . . . And tell Johnson to douse him with a few buckets of salt water."

JACK LONDON
The Sea Wolf (1904)

But while every single player differed markedly from every other, there was a certain uniform negativeness of expression which had the effect of a mask—as if they had all eaten of the same root that for the time compelled the brains of each to the same narrow monotony of action.

GEORGE ELIOT
Daniel Deronda (1876)

————•◆•————

After returning home one night from the club where he had lost all the money he had on him, he found when undressing a bank-note he had overlooked. At once he put on his clothes again, late though it was, and wandering the streets till he found a coffee-house still open where the customers were playing dominoes. There he remained gambling till daybreak.

STEPHAN ZWEIG
Four-and-Twenty Hours in a Woman's Life (1926)
translated by Eden and Cedar Paul

I had lost everything then, absolutely everything . . . As I was leaving the casino I looked, there was still one gulden in my vest pocket: "Ah, so there's money for my dinner!" I thought. But then, having walked a hundred more paces, I changed my mind and went back to the casino.

FYODOR DOSTOEVSKY
The Gambler (1867)
translated by Victor Terras

8

Two Cents' Worth

From Mavens, Maestros, Metaphysicians, Moralists, and Others

For most men (till by losing render'd sager)
Will back their own opinions with a wager.

GEORGE GORDON, LORD BYRON
Beppo (1818)

"**C**ontrol yourself, that's the main thing," Dostoevsky wrote in a letter to his long-suffering wife, illustrating one problem with the advice gamblers give about gambling: One can know a thing perfectly well and do just the opposite.

There has never been any shortage of advice about gambling. Every racetrack has its touts or tipsters, and there's always a 1-900 number you can call for the winners. If you've read this far you know this is not a how-to book, or a book with advice on winning craps or beating the slots or the roulette wheel. There are hundreds of such books, and if you believe one word of them I would be happy to recommend a good real estate broker who's selling plots of the Everglades dirt cheap.

The odds and ins-and-outs of any gambling game can and should be studied; there are books by experts that can help with all this, but Solomon the Wise couldn't make you a favorite at the slots, roulette, or at craps, short of teaching you how to gaff a wheel or slip in shaved "ace-six-flats" dice at the craps.

But while there are a few golden tips offered in this section about how to maximize one's winnings in games combining skill and chance, most of what these gamblers have to say about gambling has less to do with the fine points of games themselves than with the personal aspects of gambling. The emphasis here is on advice about how to conduct yourself when gambling, whether winning or losing: about character, about knowing how to "clock" others' "speed" and, most importantly, one's own. About when to go full throttle ahead and when to apply the brakes. No easy matter: As the wise Lao-tzu says, "The right moment, so hard to find, so easy to lose." Inevitably in collecting these quotations I have come across descriptions of gamblers on wretched tilts that hit me with the shock of recognition: Hey, I resemble that remark! Such passages always contain advice that one would do well to listen to and reflect upon.

A Note on Nay-Sayers

The best throw of the dice is to throw them out.

POPULAR NAY-SAYERS' EXPRESSION

In the earliest stories and chants of nearly every culture one finds accounts of prodigious wagering. Not much later one finds nay-sayers, whose very crusades to regulate gamblers argue the seemingly innate human "itch for play." To read the *Code of Manu* (c. A.D. 100)—"Let the King prohibit gambling and betting in his kingdom, for these are the vices that destroy the kingdoms of princes"—is to picture a kingdom made up of would-be gambling degenerates from top to bottom, betting on camel races, scorpion fights, and any- and everything else.

It is worth noting in this context that there has generally been much doubleness in the official attitudes toward gambling, and that with the growth of civil society this double-ness has only increased. There is both the old sense of gambling as socially dangerous, and a more recent desire to use the personal rights of individuals to gamble as a way of funding social institutions (the Jamestown colony and Harvard College, for instance, were founded on money raised by lotteries). This double attitude finds succinct expression in the following exchange in *Casablanca:*

> CAPTAIN LOUIS RENAULT: I am shocked, *shocked* to find that gambling is going on here.
>
> EMIL: Your winnings, sir.
>
> CAPTAIN RENAULT: Oh, thank you very much.
>
> > PHILIP EPSTEIN AND HOWARD KOCH (SCREENWRITERS)
> > *Casablanca* (1942)

It's not luck—there's probably no such thing as luck, and if there is you can't depend on it. All you can do is play the percentages, play your best game, and when that critical bet comes—in every money game there is always a critical bet— you hold your stomach tight and you push hard. That's the clutch. And that's where your born loser loses.

BERT
in Walter Tevis
The Hustler (1959)

———◆———

Casinos don't like to use the word "gambling" anymore. The euphemism of choice is "gaming." But you're not there to play games. You're there to gamble, with all the inherent risks. Don't be fooled by the casino's little word games.

JOHN GOLLEHON
A Gambler's Little Instruction Book (1994)

———◆———

Never mix cards and whisky unless you were weaned on Irish poteen.

MARGARET MITCHELL
Gone with the Wind (1936)

What do you do when you are pushing your luck beyond its limits? You must behave like a good philosopher and ask what axiom you must infer that you are acting under . . . If the axiom which you are acting under is not designed to make you money, you may find that your real objective at the end of the game is something else: you may be trying to prove yourself beloved of God. You must then ask yourself if—financially and emotionally—you can afford the potential rejection.

DAVID MAMET
"Things I Have Learned Playing Poker on the Hill" (1986)

———•◆•———

"Son, no matter how far you travel, or how smart you get, always remember this: Some day, somewhere, a guy is going to come to you and show you a nice brand-new deck of cards on which the seal is never broken, and this guy is going to offer to bet you that the jack of spades will jump out of this deck and squirt cider in your ear. But, son, do not bet him, for as sure as you do you are going to get an ear full of cider."

DAMON RUNYON
"The Idylls of Miss Sarah Brown" (1947)

An intelligent man gambles because this is a means of surrendering himself and his fortunes to the fates before tasting his wits and nerve. He does this because it improves the flavor of living. Unless he can do this happily, and with grace, he is a loser whether he leaves the game a richer man or a poorer. Unless he can do this, he should not gamble at all.

NICK "THE GREEK" DANDALOS
quoted in Ted Thackrey Jr., *Gambling Secrets of Nick the Greek* (1968)

Winning isn't going to change your life. So don't bet so much that you can get hurt. If that's what betting is all about for you, wear dog tags so they know where to ship the body.

LARRY MERCHANT
The National Football Lottery (1973)

Don't let losing streaks embitter you, or winning streaks carry you away. There's nine more tomorrow.
Don't fall in love with a horse, or a style.
Don't lose yourself in betting, or you're gone.

BRENDAN BOYD
Racing Days (1987)

Don't let anyone ruin your fun when gambling. More importantly, don't ruin it yourself.

JOHN GOLLEHON
A Gambler's Little Instruction Book (1994)

———•◆•———

If he be young and unskillful
plays for shekels of silver and gold
take his money my son praising Allah
the fool was made to be sold.

HAFIZ (D. 1389)
quoted in Franz Rosenthal, *Gambling in Islam* (1975)

———•◆•———

The trick always, in taking a sucker, is to get him to suggest a bet.

MARTY REISMAN
The Money Player (1974)

———•◆•———

I returned and saw under the sun, that the race is not to the swift, nor the battle to the strong . . . but time and chance happeneth to them all.

ECCLESIASTES 9:11–12

The race is not always to the swift, nor the battle to the strong—but that's the way to bet.

DAMON RUNYON (1884–1946)

Always remember, the first thing a gambler has to do is make friends with himself. A lot of people go through this world thinking they're someone else. There are a lot of players sitting at this table with mistaken identities.

PUG PEARSON
quoted in Jon Bradshaw, *Fast Company* (1975)

If you put a "d" in front of "anger," you get "danger"! In poker, the two are synonymous.

BOBBY BALDWIN
Tales Out of Tulsa (1984)

As soon as you can accept the possibility of losing philosophically, you automatically improve your chances of winning.

DARWIN ORTIZ
Casino Gambling for the Clueless (1986)

Don't be suckered into making "sucker" bets, unless, of course, you don't know the difference, in which case you're a sucker anyhow.

> JOHN GOLLEHON
> *A Gambler's Little Instruction Book* (1994)

———◆———

Sometimes the best way to get up a game is to walk in from nowhere and make a preposterous claim about how good you are and aggravate people into challenging you for high stakes. That's called hoorah. You hoorah someone into playing.

> DON WILLIS
> quoted in John Grissim, *Billiards* (1979)

———◆———

Play not with dice: no, cultivate thy corn-land. Enjoy the gain, and deem that wealth sufficient.
There are thy cattle, there thy wife, O gambler.

> "PRAYER OF A GAMBLER"
> *Rig Veda*

So intermix your care with joy, you may
Lighten your labour by a little play.

> FROM THE LATIN
> in Charles Cotton
> *The Compleate Gamester* (1674)

———◆·———

Play not for gain, but sport. Who plays for more
Than he can lose with pleasure, stakes his heart
Perhaps his wife's too, and whom she hath bore.

> GEORGE HERBERT
> *Temple: Church Porch* (1633)

———◆·———

I do advise all persons of quality never to play for more than
they might throw away on any other diversion; and those of a
lower rank not to lose more at a time than they can bear,
without a detriment to their affairs.

> THEOPHILUS LUCUS, ESQ.
> *Memoirs of the Lives, Intrigues, and Comical Adventures of the Most
> Famous Gamesters and Celebrated Sharpers* (1714)

———◆·———

Don't pursue a career as a nine-ball player if you have a weak
heart!

> STEVE MIZERAK WITH MICHAEL E. PANOZZO
> *Play Better Pool* (1998)

Strong players will sooner raise than call.

> AVERY CARDOZA
> *How to Play Winning Poker* (1987)

———◆———

Predictable play is costly in poker.

> AVERY CARDOZA
> *How to Play Winning Poker* (1987)

———◆———

In order to show a profit you have to leave the table.

> DARWIN ORTIZ
> *Casino Gambling for the Clueless* (1986)

———◆———

My father once told me never to bet on anything but Notre Dame and the Yankees.

> NEW JERSEY GOVERNOR BRENDAN BYRNE
> cutting ribbon to open Resorts Casino

———◆———

Let me advise you, if you play (when your business will permit) let not a covetous desire of winning another's money engage you to be losing your own.

> CHARLES COTTON
> *The Compleate Gamester* (1674)

So I learned how to win a little at a time, but finally I learned this: If you're too careful, your whole life can become a fucking grind.

DAVID LEVIEN AND BRIAN KOPPLEMAN (SCREENWITERS)
Rounders (1998)

———◆———

There are persons who are constantly pursued by bad luck. To such I say—*never play.*

GEROLAMO CARDANO
The Book on Games of Chance (c. 1520)

———◆———

You better learn to plug up your leaks or you'll be broke . . . You really get to see the person when you're gambling with them.

CHIP REESE
quoted in Timothy L. O'Brien, *Bad Bet* (1998)

———◆———

During a hot roll at a crap table a Southerner leaned over and shook a fist of encouragement at me. "Cut ya sef a new piece a bait," he said, "and fish a little deeper."

LARRY MERCHANT
The National Football Lottery (1973)

"Don't swim beyond your depth, though."

> DOLOHOV TO ROSTOV
> in Leo Tolstoy
> *War and Peace* (1869)

———— ◆ ————

A lot of good players never get to the top because when they get ahead in a game they start feeling sorry for their opponent. They ease up on him instead of kicking him when he is down . . . You've got to look at it this way: If you are playing your grandmother a fifty-point game, try to beat her fifty to nothing.

> DAN McGOORTY
> as told to Robert Bryne, *McGoorty* (1972)

———— ◆ ————

"Watch 'em from two tables away, fine," says Knish, "But don't sit down with them."

> DAVID LEVIEN AND BRIAN KOPPLEMAN (SCREENWRITERS)
> *Rounders* (1998)

———— ◆ ————

If you're in a card game and you don't know who the sucker is, you're it.

> POKER SAYING

If the action's there, keep it there.

POOL SAYING

———◆———

Eat your betting money but don't bet your eating money.

HORSERACING PROVERB

———◆———

Never bet on anything that talks.

GAMBLING ADAGE

———◆———

If you play fast you can't last; and if you play slow you're bound to go.

POPULAR SAYING

Timing equals freedom or greater chances for movement.

SCRIBBLED IN A BACKGAMMON BOOK

IN THE HOUSE OF BACKGAMMON

———◆———

It's as important to make good folds in poker as it is to make good bets . . . The biggest mistake weak players make is playing too many hands.

AVERY CARDOZA
How to Play Winning Poker (1987)

Aces are larger than life and greater than mountains.

> MIKE CARO
> quoted in Doyle Brunson
> *How I Made $1,000,000 Playing Poker* (1979)

———◆———

I cheat my boys every chance I get. I want to make 'em sharp.

> WILLIAM AVERY ROCKEFELLER (C. 1850)
> (John D.'s father)

———◆———

When Franklin D. Roosevelt told all the citizens the only thing to fear is fear itself, he wasn't giving them any soft con. Fear is a hideous thing. It's a malignancy of the mind and the soul and if it really gets to you, it can turn your life into a deadly horror. Fear can make a sucker do some of the most drastic things you ever imagined . . . like taking a job.

> MINNESOTA FATS WITH TOM FOX
> *The Great Bank Shot and Other Robberies* (1966)

So use all that is called Fortune. Most men gamble with her, and gain all, and lose all, as her wheel rolls . . . In the Will work and acquire, and thou hast chained the wheel of Chance, and shalt always drag her after thee.

RALPH WALDO EMERSON
"Self-Reliance" (1841)

———•◆•———

Many bad players will not improve because they cannot bear self-knowledge . . . The bad player will not deign to determine what he thinks by watching what he does. To do so might . . . reveal a need to be abused (in calling what must be a superior hand); a need to be loved (in staying in for "that one magic card"); a need to have Daddy relent (in trying to bluff out the obvious best hand); et cetera . . . It's not easy to face that, rather than playing cards in spite of our losses, we are playing cards because of them.

DAVID MAMET
"Things I Have Learned Playing Poker on the Hill" (1986)

And once or twice to throw the dice
Is a gentlemanly game,
But he does not win who plays with sin,
In the secret House of Shame.

> OSCAR WILDE
> *The Ballad of Reading Gaol* (1898)

———•◆•———

Bluff enough to get called half the time.

> GEORGE COFFIN
> *The Poker Game Complete* (1950)

———•◆•———

Another will light a cigarette and pretend not to know when his turn comes to bet; then after glancing around the tables, he bets. He has them.

> HERBERT O. YARDLEY
> *The Education of a Poker Player* (1957)

———•◆•———

Never play cards with a man named Doc.

> NELSON ALGREN (1909–81)

As much is lost by a card too many as a card too few.

MIGUEL DE CERVANTES
Don Quixote (1615)

———•◆•———

Put not your trust in Kings and Princes:
Three of a kind will take them both.

ROBERT C. SCHENCK
Rules for Playing Poker (1880)

———•◆•———

Patience, and shuffle the cards.

MIGUEL DE CERVANTES
Don Quixote (1615)

———•◆•———

One should always play fair when one has the winning cards.

OSCAR WILDE (1854–1900)

———•◆•———

Decide on three things at the start: the rules of the game, the stakes, and the quitting time.

CHINESE PROVERB

Beat him, eat him and get out.

> RICHARD PRICE (SCREENWRITER)
> *The Color of Money* (1986)

———◆———

"Thank you, I would like a banana," is the most you should tell your opponent.

> PHIL SIMBORG
> "Simborg's Laws of Backgammon" (1998)

———◆———

Going to the bathroom during a poker or dice game is a mistake. You might miss a hot hand worth a hundred thousand, and nothing in the bathroom is worth that much.

> NICK "THE GREEK" DANDALOS
> quoted in Cy Rice, *Nick the Greek: King of Gamblers* (1969)

———◆———

Stake your counter as boldly every whit,
Venture as warily, use the same skill,
Do your best, whether winning or losing it,
If you chose to play.

> ROBERT BROWNING
> "Love among the Ruins" (1851)

A wise player ought to accept his throws and score them, not bewail his luck.

> SOPHOCLES (C. 496–406 B.C.)
> *Phaedra*

———•◆•———

You shall allow wagers to run high enough so that courage is shown and felt, but not so high that retribution can be excused by an excessive folly.

> JACK RICHARDSON
> *Memoir of a Gambler* (1979)

———•◆•———

What are hunches but mysterious messages coming out of the deeps of our minds through some sort of mental telepathy?

> HAROLD S. SMITH SR. WITH JOHN WESLEY NOBLE
> *I Want to Quit Winners* (1961)

———•◆•———

I'd sooner play against one than on one.

> NICK "THE GREEK" DANDALOS ON HUNCHES
> quoted in Cy Rice, *Nick the Greek: King of Gamblers* (1969)

I don't believe in hunches. Hunches are for dogs making love.

AMARILLO SLIM
quoted in Jon Bradshaw, *Fast Company* (1975)

Take calculated risks. That is quite different from being rash.

GENERAL GEORGE S. PATTON (1885–1945)

"Some people lose their heads cold sober. Cards, dice, pool; it makes no difference. You want to make a living that way, you want to be a winner, you got to keep your head. And you got to remember that there's a loser somewhere in you, whining at you, and you got to learn to cut his water off."

BERT
in Walter Tevis
The Hustler (1959)

Knowing how to figure the odds will not make a winning player. But a total disregard of the odds for a long period will surely make a loser. Lucky players don't last.

A. D. LIVINGSTON
Poker Strategy and Winning Play (1971)

Mathematics . . . are a good servant to the poker player but a bad master.

HUBERT PHILLIPS
Profitable Poker (1960)

———•◆•———

You get a tell by the way they move their checks. You get the reaction, the conversation . . . watch the veins in his neck, watch his eyes, the way he sweats.

JOHNNY MOSS, WORLD-CHAMPION POKER PLAYER
quoted in Jon Bradshaw
Fast Company (1975)

———•◆•———

"My advice was to go home. It's still to go home." He said it in a way that made me both like him and despise him. It was the gentlest sentiment that could have been offered, and at the same time it was wholly ignorant of the condition I was in, it ignored everything—the losses, the excitement, the hope, the desperation, the high. All of it. It was nonsense, a Hallmark card.

FREDRICK BARTHELME
Bob the Gambler (1997)

Make up your mind what the other man's hole card is, otherwise he will decide what yours is!

> ERIC STEINER
> quoted in David Spanier, *Total Poker* (1977)

———•◆•———

It's necessary to crawl into an opponent's mind—deep, deep inside—and decide whether he holds a strong or a weak hand. In order to do this, you must learn to feel. Feel his pain, agony, hope, desperation.

> MIKE CARO
> *Mike Caro's Book of Tells* (1984)

———•◆•———

Remember that Fortune does not like people to be overjoyed at her favours, and that she prepares bitter deceptions for the imprudent, who are intoxicated by success.

> ANDREW STEINMETZ
> *The Gaming Table* (1870)

9

Games People Play

Gambling, betting on horse, among other things, is a way of life. The manner in which a man chooses to gamble indicates his character or his lack of it.

WILLIAM SAROYAN (1908–81)

Before you conquer the three rebellious ivory balls and make them do your bidding, you must first conquer yourself. I have found billiards to be more than a game; I have found it to be a philosophy of self-control.

WILLIE HOPPE
Thirty Years of Billiards (1925)

Among the seemingly endless kinds of contests refined in nineteenth-century America for the purpose of making a friendly wager now and then, poker, craps, pocket pool, and horse racing have emerged most distinctively as national institutions. Each has its eccentric types, characters, and settings made famous in literature, cinema, and song. And each has made lively contributions to American speech, poker idioms especially. The homespun "you betchu," for instance, began as a clipped form of the frontier poker question, "How much do you bet?" And twentieth-century presidents can't seem to resist describing social programs in term of hands dealt by the government to the people. So we've received a Square Deal (Teddy Roosevelt), a New Deal (Franklin Delano Roosevelt), a Fair Deal (Harry Truman), and quite a few raws deals between and since.

The quotations in this section suggest some of the flavor and spirit of four great American pastimes. (The games we choose to gamble at have something to tell us about ourselves. Blackjack players, for instance, tend to sit and brood, while crapaholics stand and yell.) The essence of poker, which entered the country as *poque* and traveled upriver from New Orleans (to Cincinnati, "Poker-Polis"), and then out West, is calculation and bluff. "The art of civilized bushwhacking," Nick the Greek calls it, poker is about sizing up, outfoxing, and fleecing your fellow players, and naturally appeals to businessmen and politicians. Craps, which was developed by

African-Americans in the Mississippi valley, follows Vedic, Roman, and European dicing in its passion for gamble, and attracts purists and aficianados of chance, whether flamboyant high rollers or bottom-dollar stoics. Poolrooms in the early twentieth century became cool illicit alternative social centers. (My favorite name for one is the TIME AND A HALF POOL ROOM in Toni Morrison's novel *Sula*.) The game blends surgical care, nerve, and imaginative problem solving. It is a pursuit of excellence pitting players against the lay of the table, themselves, and an opponent who shoots back. Horse players are passionate researchers in an endless battle with uncertainty, tellers of wrenching stories of broken trifectas, devotees of the grandstand who despite hard knocks maintain their love for the feel of horses gliding into the stretch, the pounding colors of the horses surging for home. True, most have at one time or other, after wagering on a horse that got up on the wrong side of the paddock, wanted to do like Alex Carras in *Blazing Saddles,* when he KOs a horse with a short right cross. But because it generally does little good to blame or attack the horse, they tend to vent at the expense of jockeys.

Pool and Billiards

The real feeling of this game is pool itself. The stories are just to pass the feeling. Pool is the feeling. Pool is everything. If you can feel the game, that's the nuts of it right there.

DAVE ALLO
quoted in John Grissim, *Billiards* (1979)

———•◆•———

Tony hit maybe the prettiest safety I'd ever seen. It unfolded like the wings of a butterfly, the cue hitting the seven firmly a little less than half-ball, and the two balls tracing mirror-image paths around the table, the black counterclockwise, the cue ball clockwise, and they ended in almost exactly the same positions in which they had started.

DAVID McCUMBER
Off the Rail (1996)

———•◆•———

"Stay out of poolrooms, kid, or all you'll ever have is fun."

WILLIAM KENNEDY
Billy Phelan's Greatest Game (1978)

Let it alone, let's to billiards.

WILLIAM SHAKESPEARE
Antony and Cleopatra (1607)

Pool has more mental strain to it than any other game, I think, except maybe chess. Certainly more pressure than anything involving physical effort. In football when you make that first contact you lose a lot of the doggishness you might have. But with pool nobody ever whacks you, so your nerves just keep building, and you gotta keep it all inside.

JIM REMPE
quoted in John Grissim, *Billiards* (1979)

The masse shot of Jacob Schaefer, Sr. was so brilliant that it was mentioned in his 1910 obituary in the *New York Times*.

MIKE SHAMOS
Pool: History, Strategies, and Legends (1994)

His stroking arm was like a conscious thing, and the cue stick was a living extension of it. There were nerves in the wood of it, and he could feel the tapping of the leather tip with the nerves, could feel the balls roll; and the exquisite sound that they made as they hit the bottoms of the pockets was a sound both there, on the table, and in the very center of his soul.

WALTER TEVIS
The Hustler (1959)

———•◆•———

I watch him for an hour—if he misses more than one shot I know I can beat him.

LUTHER "WIMPY" LASSITER, CHAMPION POOL PLAYER
quoted in Mike Shamos, *Pool: History, Strategies, and Legends* (1994)

———•◆•———

"I will be perfectly fair with you. I'll play you left-handed." I felt hurt, for he was cross-eyed, freckled, and had red hair, and I determined to teach him a lesson. He won first shot, ran out, took my half dollar, and all I got was the opportunity to chalk my cue.

"If you can play like that with your left hand," I said, "I'd like to see you play with your right hand."

"I can't," he said. "I'm left-handed."

MARK TWAIN
speech at billiards exhibition (1906)

To play billiards well is a sign of a misspent youth.

> HERBERT SPENCER
> *Life and Letters of Spencer* (1899)

———◆———

The entertainment industry's best-ever pool player . . . which is hardly surprising in view of his fantastic co-ordination, was Fred Astaire.

> NED POLSKY
> *Hustlers, Beats, and Others* (1998)

———◆———

To me pool is an art. If nobody'll pay me to be artistic with it, tough, I'll find a way. Look, if nobody woulda fed Michelangelo he still would have painted his pictures and sculpted his statues—and robbed people to continue doing what his love was.

> DAVE ALLO
> quoted in John Grissim, *Billiards* (1979)

"I can have self-respect doing something besides shooting pool."

"No you can't," Fats said. "Not you."

"Why not? I didn't sign a contract that says I shoot pool for life."

"It's been signed for you."

> Fats and Fast Eddie
> in Walter Tevis
> *The Color of Money* (1984)

Gambling and pool have been joined like two balls frozen on the end rail.

> David McCumber
> *Off the Rail* (1996)

By an act of will or of flight he focused his whole awareness on the game he played. His mind undertook it with intent concentration. He took pride in little two-cushion banks, little triumphs of accuracy, small successes of foresight.

> Wallace Stegner
> "The Blue-Winged Teal" (1950)

He remembered the feeling of power he had had, running the table, his eye, brains, arm, all of him concentrated on the balls, all clicking together like a coordinated machine, and the thrill that went with each shot as the balls were smashed, cut, banked, eased into the pockets.

> JAMES T. FARRELL
> *The Young Manhood of Studs Lonnigan* (1934)

————•◆•————

Play with a house cue for now . . . you walk in with that nobody'd go near you with a nickel.

> FAST EDDIE
> in Richard Price (screenwriter)
> *The Color of Money* (1986)

————•◆•————

Billiards possesses an infinite storehouse of engaging challenges, of marvelous patterns of spheres in motion limited only by a man's imagination.

> JOHN GRISSIM
> *Billiards* (1979)

I try to beat a game, half chance, half-cold
and steady practice, struggling for the skill
that might kill chance.

HENRY TAYLOR
"An Afternoon of Pocket Billiards" (1975)

Power over the cue ball, over the object ball, is power over
ourselves. It is the sweetest irony that pool has gathered the
reputation of being a game for louts and idlers, when, to be
played well, it demands such incredible discipline of movement, of thinking, of emotion.

DAVID MCCUMBER
Off the Rail (1997)

Now gently, now hard he played the ball, seemingly at random, and each time, as it caromed off the other two, for him
brought forth a new geometric pattern from the green void,
making a starry heaven. Cue ball kissing white ball over
green felt, red ball over green felt, bringing tracks into being
. . . Often he played for as long as a half-hour with only one
ball, white over the green surface, a solitary star in the sky.

HEINRICH BOLL
Billiards at Half Past Nine (1962)

Imagination plays its part, too, in the game of pocket billiards, just as it does in any sport.

> WILLIE MOSCONI
> *Mosconi on Pocket Billiards* (1948)

———•◆•———

His control of cueball speed was so beautiful I drool when I think of it.

> SHORT GORDON
> on Dan McGoorty
> in Don McGoorty and Robert Byrne, *McGoorty* (1972)

———•◆•———

Up, all of us, and to billiards.

> SAMUEL PEPYS
> *Diary* (July 17, 1665)

Some even find that the game of billiards develops courage, a sharp and steady eye, and good aim, and doctors assert that this game is extremely beneficial to unbalanced men.

MIKHAIL ZOSHCHENKO
"A Jolly Game" (1938)

———•◆•———

The noble game of billiards is peculiarly in harmony with the mechanical genius of our people; it combines science with gymnastics, teaching the eye to judge distances, the mind to calculate forces, and the arm to execute; it expands the chest while giving grace and elegance to the form, and it affords even to the illiterate a practical basis for the appreciation of mathematical and geometric truth . . .

MICHAEL PHELAN
The Game of Billiards (1858)

Poker and Cards

POKER, n. A game said to be played with cards for some purpose to this lexicographer unknown.

> AMBROSE BIERCE
> *The Devil's Dictionary* (1906)

———•◆•———

The first rule of poker, whether you play by western or eastern rules, is put up or shut up!

> HENRY FONDA
> in *A Big Hand for the Little Lady* (1966)

———•◆•———

Cards are war, in disguise of a sport.

> CHARLES LAMB
> *Essays of Elia* (1832)

———•◆•———

Poker and American history are inseparable.

> JOHN MCDONALD
> *Strategy in Poker, Business, and War* (1950)

Poker is . . . a fascinating, wonderful, intricate adventure on the high seas of human nature.

DAVID A. DANIEL
Poker: How to Win at the Great American Game (1997)

Skill can often qualify bad luck at poker.

ERIC AMBLER
Passage of Arms (1959)

I am going to say something about the great American game—draw poker. It stands alone, in a class by itself. If it have a peer, 'tis the game of life. Life itself is but a gamble. I am not a gambler, but most real cowmen or punchers I ever knew could play good enough to lose.

OSCAR RUSH (1930)

There are few things that are so unpardonably neglected in our country as poker. The upper class knows very little about it. Now and then you find ambassadors who have sort of a general knowledge of the game, but the ignorance of the people is fearful. Why, I have known clergymen, good men, kind-hearted, liberal, sincere, and all that, who did not know the meaning of a "flush." It is enough to make one ashamed of the species.

MARK TWAIN (1835–1910)

Owing largely to the bluff, poker has influenced our thinking on life, love, business, and even war. In fact, the mathematical theory of games . . . was given a high security classification by the armed services during World War II!

A. D. LIVINGSTON
Poker Strategy and Winning Play (1971)

Poker is the game closest to the Western conception of life, where life and thought are recognized as intimately combined, where free will prevails over philosophies of fate or of chance, where men are considered moral agents, and where—at least in the short run—the important thing is not what happens but what people think happens.

JOHN LUKACS
"Poker and American Character" (1963)

———— •◆• ————

Poker is a game of many skills: you need card sense, psychological insight, a good memory, controlled aggression, enough mathematical know-how to work out the odds as each hand develops, and what poker players call a leather ass—i.e., patience.

ALVIN ALVAREZ
"No Limit" (1994)

———— •◆• ————

A computer could play fair-to-middling Poker. But no computer could ever stand face-to-face with a table full of people it had never met before, and make quality, high-profit decisions based on psychology.

DOYLE BRUNSON
How I Made $1,000,000 Playing Poker (1979)

I haven't played with many women who are really good at what they do. They want to invade what they think is a man's world; it's almost a personal thing, they want to beat men. I don't understand it. This is a game of talent. If you have the talent, it's not going to matter who you are.

> CISSY BOTTOMS (1996)
> quoted in Adam Platt, "Women Are Beating the Pants Off Men in the Macho World of High-Stakes Poker," *Elle* (1996)

———•◆•———

I like to play poker with politicians. They're easy to beat . . . sometimes in poker it's smarter to lose with a winning hand so that you can win later with a losing hand. Politicians can't accept that.

> ROBERT REDFORD
> in *Havana* (1990)

———•◆•———

I believe some good Poker players actually employ a degree of extrasensory perception (ESP). While I've never studied the subject in depth, it seems to me there's too much evidence to ignore that ESP exists or that most people have it to some degree.

> DOYLE BRUNSON
> *How I Made $1,000,000 Playing Poker* (1979)

Good high-stakes poker players are neither noble nor greedy. They've sized up their fellow players, know a good deal about probabilities and tendencies, and wish like poets that their most audacious moves be perceived as part of a series of credible gestures.

STEPHEN DUNN
"Gambling: Remembrances and Assertions" (1993)

The number of ways in which a player may inadvertantly tip off the strength or weakness of his hidden cards is limitless, and include such physical clues as excessive sweating, trembling hands, or a change in voice tone.

PETER O. STEINER
Thursday Night Poker (1996)

A genuine smile usually means a genuine hand; a forced smile is a bluff.

MIKE CARO
Mike Caro's Book of Tells (1984)

"How long does it take to learn poker, Dad?"
    "All your life, son."

> MICHAEL PERTWEE
> quoted in David Spanier
> *Total Poker* (1977)

———•◆•———

Lying in wait is the secret of success in poker.

> R. A. PROCTOR
> *Poker Principles and Chance Laws* (1880s)

———•◆•———

A man who can play delightfully on a guitar and keep a knife in his boot would make an excellent poker player.

> W. J. FLORENCE
> *Handbook on Poker* (1891)

———•◆•———

"In a game of poker, I can put the players' souls in my pocket."

> BEAUSOURIRE, HAITIAN POKER PLAYER
> quoted in Jack Richardson, *Memoir of a Gambler* (1979)

———•◆•———

Stud is a game for those who like their poker neat.

> JOHN MCDONALD
> *Stategy in Poker, Business, and War* (1950)

Dice and Backgammon

Alea iacta est.
  "The die is cast."

> GAIUS JULIUS CAESAR
> before crossing the Rubicon (49 B.C.)

———•◆•———

As I walk from crap game to crap game, my brain becomes active and agile and dwells on lofty thoughts.

> NICK "THE GREEK" DANDALOS
> quoted in Cy Rice, *Nick the Greek: King of Gamblers* (1969)

———•◆•———

You cannot believe the level of excitement that a craps table can generate. I've heard people make all kinds of involuntary sounds as a hot shooter rolls. One guy, a well-dressed, balding businessman, very dignified and well-mannered, suddenly started crowing like a rooster as a shooter caught fire. This guy's face became beet-red as he crowed with delight. Another man howled like a wolf one night as he won his bets. One older woman would do a little piroutte everytime her numbers hit.

> FRANK SCOBLETE
> *Beat the Craps Out of the Casinos: How to Play Craps and Win!*
> (1991)

Nathan Detroit's crap game is apt to be anywhere, because it moves about every night.

DAMON RUNYON
"Blood Pressure" (1929)

———•◆•———

Hazard is the most bewitching game that is played on the Dice; for when a man begins to play, he knows not when to leave off; and, having once accustomed himself to play at Hazard, he hardly, ever after, minds anything else.

CHARLES COTTON
The Compleate Gamester (1674)

———•◆•———

He was greatly devoted to dice, even publishing a book on the art, and he actually used to play while driving, having the board fitted to his carriage in such a way as to prevent his game from being distrurbed.

SUETONIOUS (C. 69–141)
on Claudius
Lives of the Caesers
translated by Robert Graves (1957)

Downward they roll, and then spring quickly
upward and, handless, force
The man with hands to serve them.
Cast on the board, like lumps of magic charcoal,
though themselves cold, they burn
The heart to ashes.

VEDIC HYMN, *RIG VEDA*

How many events can be crowded into the space of a second! How much depends upon the throw of a dice!

HONORÉ DE BALZAC
The Wild Ass's Skin (1831)

Backgammon is a queer compulsive game. It's the luck factor that seduces everyone into believing that they are good, that they can actually win. But that's wishful thinking. To become good, really good, at backgammon could cost you several years of your time . . . It cost me a lot. But I learned.

TIM HOLLAND, WORLD-CHAMPION BACKGAMMON PLAYER
quoted in Jon Bradshaw, *Fast Company* (1975)

In that company I debase myself for the rest of the day, playing at "cricca" and backgammon: a thousand quarrels arise, and innumerable insults are exchanged, with offensive words.

> NICCOLO MACHIAVELLI
> letter to Francesco Vettori (1513)
> translated by Shirley Hazzard

———◆———

The only athletic sport I ever mastered was backgammon.

> DOUGLAS WILLIAM JERROLD (1803–57)

———◆———

I hated all manner of gaming, except backgammon, at which my old friend and I sometimes took a two penny hit.

> OLIVER GOLDSMITH
> *The Vicar of Wakefield* (1766)

———◆———

If you're not a compulsive/addictive personality, there's no point in playing backgammon.

> PHIL SIMBORG
> "Simborg's Laws of Backgammon" (1998)

Dice have their laws, which the courts of justice cannot undo.

ST. AMBROSE (D. 397)

———◆———

No matter what energy one gives dice when they leave the hand, they still do not come to rest any more easily on the desired number.

JEAN JACQUES ROUSSEAU
quoted in David F. Bell, *Circumstances* (1993)

———◆———

Get up! You know nothing about the game; make room for better players.

ON A TAVERN WALL IN POMPEII
quoted in John Ashton, *The History of Gambling in England* (1898)

———◆———

The dice don't know who's throwing them. They can't be controlled telepathically. A three-year-old child can throw them as well as a top gambler.

NICK "THE GREEK" DANDALOS
quoted in Cy Rice, *Nick the Greek: King of Gamblers* (1969)

The same king [Rhampsinitus] descended alive beneath the earth, to what the Greeks call infernal regions, where he played at dice with the goddess Ceres, and alternately won and lost.

HERODOTUS (C. 485–425 B.C.)

———•◆•———

Gambling in my neighborhood was widespread and wide open . . . crap games were liable to spring up almost instantly in any hallway and disappear just as fast . . . I was eighteen before I learned gambling was illegal.

DARWIN ORTIZ
Gambling Scams (1984)

———•◆•———

"I like to think of the craps table as another country, with a culture all its own. I respect the culture and try not to offend its believers. Even if I think that what they believe is silly and what they do is idiotic, I gain nothing by letting them know my feelings."

THE CAPTAIN
quoted in Frank Scoblete
Beat the Craps Out of the Casino: How to Play Craps and Win!
(1991)

Horses

Betting . . . stimulates the caring glands. That is why there is so much caring at the race track.

LARRY MERCHANT
The National Football Lottery (1973)

———•◆•———

If you have one chink in your psychological armor, playing the horses will bring it out.

ANDREW BEYER
Beyer on Speed (1993)

———•◆•———

I'm confident that, sooner or later, most race tracks will have a special section reserved for degenerates.

JOHN GOLLEHON
A Gambler's Bedside Reader (1998)

I was nuts about the horses, too. There's something about it, when they come out and go up the track to the post. Sort of dancy and tight looking with the jock keeping a tight hold on them and maybe easing off a little and letting them run a little going up. Then once they were at the barrier it got me worse than anything.

ERNEST HEMINGWAY
"My Old Man" (1923)

———•◆•———

There where the course is,
Delight makes all of the one mind,
The riders upon the galloping horses,
The crowd that closes in behind.

W. B. YEATS
"At Galway Races" (1910)

When a race is to be run by such horses as these, and perhaps by others which, in like manner, according to their breed are strong for carriage and vigorous for the course, the people raise a shout and order the common horses to be withdrawn to another part of the field. The jockeys, who are boys expert in the management of horses, which they regulate by means of curb bridles, sometimes by threes and sometimes by twos, as the match is made, prepare themselves for the contest. Their chief aim is to prevent a competitor from getting before them.

WILLIAM FITZSTEPHEN (C. 1174)
translated from the Latin by John Stow

"You've seen my horses. They only need a driver who is worthy of them."

LEW WALLACE
Ben Hur (1880)

I've had jockeys stand up in the stirrups in the stretch and haul back on the reins just to beat me out of my money.

DAN MCGOORTY
as told to Robert Byrne, *McGoorty* (1972)

201

"I see Jockey Scroon do things to horses I bet on that he will have to answer for on the Judgment Day, if there is any justice at such a time."

DAMON RUNYON
"A Story Goes with It" (1931)

It is said that Groucho Marx once appeared in the offices of an executive at the MGM studio dressed in a jockey's uniform because, he said, "This is the only way you can get to see a producer these days." The story may be apocryphal, but the point is well taken. It is wearying to recall the time and emotion which adults in the movie colony devote to discussing the speed with which four-legged animals can traverse an elliptical course.

LEO ROSTEN
Hollywood: The Movie Colony, the Movie Makers (1941)

Gambling was so crucial to the economy of certain households that semi-respectable women slept with jockeys to get closer to "the horse's mouth."

MICHAEL ONDAATJE
Running in the Family (1982)

The stewards have ruled this a false start . . . and have ordered the horses back to the starting post.

> GEORGE SEATON, ROBERT PIROSH, AND GEORGE OPPENHEIMER (SCREEN-WRITERS)
> Marx Brothers, *A Day at the Races* (1937)

———•◆•———

If you could call the thing a horse. If it hadn't shown a flash of speed in the straight, it would have got mixed up with the next race.

> P. G. WODEHOUSE
> *Very Good, Jeeves* (1930)

———•◆•———

Nobody ever committed suicide who had a good two-year-old in the barn.

> RACETRACK SAYING

———•◆•———

Horse sense is a good judgement which keeps horses from betting on people.

> W. C. FIELDS (1880–1946)

"I am such a guy as will always listen to a tip on a horse if a story goes with the tip. In fact, I will not give you a nickel for a tip without a story, but it must be a first-class story, and most horse players are the same way."

> DAMON RUNYON
> "A Story Goes with It" (1931)

———— •◆• ————

Last Hope cannot walk a mile and a quarter, which is the Derby distance, let alone run that far, and . . . even if Last Hope can run a mile and a quarter, he cannot run it fast enough to get up a sweat.

> DAMON RUNYON
> "It Comes Up Mud" (1931)

———— •◆• ————

I went to the race track once in my life and I bet on a horse called Battlegun and all the horses come out and mine is the only horse in the race with training wheels.

> WOODY ALLEN
> *Monologue*

Now I bent to the charts like an adept parsing mystical texts. Sometimes they were runic, impossible to decipher, but other times winners stepped readily forward to speak their names.

BILL BARICH
Laughing in the Hills (1980)

———◆———

I especially love the talk about why a particular horse can't lose. When that horse loses we're left sometimes with pure intelligence, a fine mind that we've been privileged to overhear, however wrong.

STEPHEN DUNN
"Gambling: Remembrances and Assertions" (1993)

———◆———

The Racing Form—that poor man's anthology of histories, equine and human—provides the kind of information that instructs us about the insufficiency of certain knowledge.

STEPHEN DUNN
"Gambling: Remembrances and Assertions" (1993)

The track was sloppy, and we might as well have thrown darts at the program.

JOHN GOLLEHON
A Gambler's Bedside Reader (1998)

———————•◆•———————

At the racetrack, most judgements made are faulty; as many as possible must be laid off on surrogates. Fact and opinion blend seamlessly at the track.

BRENDAN BOYD
Racing Days (1987)

———————•◆•———————

The way his horses ran could be summed up in a word. Last.

He once had a horse who finished ahead of the winner of the 1942 Kentucky Derby.

Unfortunately, the horse started running in the 1941 Kentucky Derby.

GROUCHO MARX
Esquire (1972)

"Those are racehorses, aren't they?"

"That's right," Bert said.

"They look like any other horses to me."

Bert laughed. "What other kind of horses does a pool hustler see, anyway—except racehorses?"

WALTER TEVIS
The Hustler (1959)

———•◆•———

Even during the war the August races were not to be postponed. Ceylon could have been invaded during the late afternoon as most of the Light Infantry was at the race track during those hours.

MICHAEL ONDAATJE
Running in the Family (1982)

———•◆•———

we are betting on the miracle again
there before the purple mountains,
as the horses parade past
so much more beautiful than
our lives.

CHARLES BUKOWSKI
"12 minutes to post"
Betting on the Muse (1996)

"I do not think I will ever bet on anything Jockey Scroon rides if they pay off in advance."

> DAMON RUNYON
> "A Story Goes with It" (1931)

———•◆•———

Gwine to run all night!
Gwine to run all day!
I'll bet my money on de bobtail nag—
Somebody bet on de bay.

> STEPHEN COLLINS FOSTER
> "Camptown Races" (1850)

Then they went out of sight again and then they came pounding out and down the hill and all going nice and sweet and easy and taking the fence smooth in a bunch, and moving away from us all solid. Looked as though you could walk across their backs they were all so bunched and smooth.

> ERNEST HEMINGWAY
> "My Old Man"

———•◆•———

For full-time gamblers, time loses more than its context at the track. Post time is one. Tuesdays are dark. What else matters?

> BRENDAN BOYD
> *Racing Days* (1987)

10

The Company We Keep

A Gallery of Hustlers, Kibbitzers, High Rollers, Handicappers, Suckers, and Other Citizens of the Republic of Chance

That's what they call the great pyramid of gamblin'. Sharks at the top, then the rounders, the minnows, and at the bottom the fish—the suckers, the suppliers. Scavengers and suppliers, just like in life.

> PUG PEARSON
> quoted in Jon Bradshaw
> *Fast Company* (1975)

The racetrack doesn't create eccentrics, it attracts them. But it does little to curb their quirks once they're there. It fosters idiosyncracies, encourages traits we'd temper elsewhere. People become cartoon versions of themselves at the track. It's a license to act inappropriately.

> BRENDAN BOYD
> *Racing Days* (1987)

In most action places I have known—poolrooms, chess and backgammon houses or park tables, poker parlors, floating craps games, OTBs, thoroughbred, trotter, or dog tracks, jai alai frontons, table-tennis parlors, casinos—the clientele is about as representative a cross section of the adult male population of the neighborhood, city, or region you're in as you're likely to find. (Women increasingly frequent these places, especially casinos, but there's not equal involvement yet on that front—at various times and places, though, it should be noted that it has been socially acceptable for women to gamble voraciously.) People of every ethnicity and class rub shoulders with one another in what John Grissim calls a kind of "cultural halfway house," ex-cons negotiating settlements between lawyers, with weapons and degrees checked at the door.

In places where the people play not against a common enemy (the House with its oppressive edge or vigorish) but against one another, players fall into types and/or positions on the gambler's food chain, sharks (con artists) naturally feeding on fish ("live ones" full of faulty self-perceptions). "I could not win a lot of money as long as the original idea was mine," writes table-tennis hustler Marty Reisman, suggesting that the mark plays a sizable role in sharking himself.

In an action place the qualities most valued are basic decency (i.e., paying your debts, being a decent loser), gamble (not, finally, fattening up on the compulsively self-deceived), wit (in some contexts you can lose the wager but prevail in the conversation), and excellence. No one in an action place cares about the background of a good gambler. A priori ideas about newcomers may be quickly abandoned: On first sight the judge who lives on Madison Avenue is probably a cheapskate and a pigeon, a millionaire who sweats over three dollars and deserves to be plucked; but after a session or two he'll be judged by how he gambles, how he acts, and if he stays he'll probably be rechristened. Basic unwritten codes of conduct are enforced as well. Like, when you lose you fork over, and if you're going to kibbitz a game you okay it with the players, know when your two cents' worth is called for, and when you should keep your trap shut.

Action places are about people as much as gamble—people with a shared fellowship in gamble. About the company we keep.

They are creatures of contradictions—they are fiercely greedy, lavishly generous, wary in many things, reckless of life, ready to take any advantage, yet possessed of a diseased sense of honour.

JAMES RUNCIMAN
Side Lights (1893)

Gambling is an enchanting witchery . . . [the gambler] is either lifted up to the top of mad joy with success, or plunged to the bottom of despair by misfortune, always in extremes, always in a storm . . . Restless I call him, because (such is the itch of play) either winning or losing he can never be satisfied, if he wins he thinks to win more, if he loses he hopes to recover.

CHARLES COTTON
The Compleate Gamester (1674)

When I told Canada Bill the game he was playing in was crooked, he said, "I know it is, but it's the only game in town."

GEORGE DEVOL
Forty Years a Gambler on the Mississippi (1892)

All his life juices, energies, violence, boldness have gone into roulette . . . He is a poet in his own way, but the fact is he is ashamed of that poetry, because he feels profoundly its baseness, although the need for risk in fact ennobles it in his own eyes.

> FYODOR DOSTOEVSKY
> letter to Nikolay Strakhov (September 30, 1863)
> on the idea for *The Gambler*
> *Complete Letters* (1988)

———•◆•———

I have slept less than any man who ever lived.

> NICK "THE GREEK" DANDALOS
> quoted in J. Philip Jones, *Gambling Yesterday and Today* (1973)

———•◆•———

You can't gamble by the clock . . . Time can place a limitation on pleasure.

> NICK "THE GREEK" DANDALOS
> quoted in Cy Rice, *Nick the Greek: King of Gamblers* (1969)

The Casino Manager got on the loudspeaker system and announced, "A bomb threat has been received; please vacate the casino." Nobody moved. Five minutes later the Casino Manager announced again, "Please everybody leave the casino. A bomb threat has been received."

The blackjack players were the first to go, then the crap shooters . . . then the baccarat players; finally the roulette players left. But the slot machines kept whirring and flashing.

> MARIO PUZO
> *Inside Las Vegas* (1976)

———— ◆ ————

"Good afternoon, gentlemen . . . what's the name of this game?"

> KIRK DOUGLAS
> in Leon Uris (screenwriter)
> *Gunfight at the O.K. Corral* (1957)

———— ◆ ————

I was attending high school during the day, and this elite postgraduate school at night, where the action was designed to move faster than the players' eyes.

> JIMMY "THE GREEK" SNYDER
> *Jimmy the Greek, by Himself* (1975)
> with Mickey Herskowitz and Steve Perkins

There is the challenge of self-control, of calculating coolness and unshakability in the face of wildly fluctuating fortunes and the mercilessness of chance. This is a virtue men have always sought, and gambling, more than any other test of "grace under pressure" besides actual combat—puts it on the line.

DON ETHAN MILLER
The Book of Jargon (1981)

Somewhere along the road, the pros have lost their sense of urgency. Their lives are one long poker game, which begins when they turn professional and will end—if it ever ends— when they retire.

ALVIN ALVAREZ
"No Limit" (1994)

The first of the successful systems players . . . was a colorful individual known as "Greasy John." Large and obese, he acquired his name from his habit of coming to the casino with a large bag of very greasy fried chicken . . . Since Greasy John's hands were generally dripping with chicken fat, the cards soon became too oily to handle comfortably.

EDWARD O. THORP
Beat the Dealer (1962)

They have a Dixie Cup full of nickels or dimes in the left hand and an Iron Boy work glove on the right hand to keep the calluses from getting sore. Every time they pull the handle, the machine makes a sound much like the sound a cash register makes before the bell rings . . . The whole sound keeps churning up and over and over again in eccentric series all over the place, like one of those random-sound radio symphonies by John Cage.

TOM WOLFE
The Kandy-Kolored Tangerine-Flake Streamline Baby (1965)

I don't care what Gallup or Harris says, tell me what Jimmy the Greek says.

JIM BERRY
cartoon

You can be as wise as Solomon, with the most iron character and still lose control.

FYODOR DOSTOEVSKY
letter to Varvara Konstant (September 1, 1863)
Complete Letters (1988)
translated by David A. Lowe

The gambler is quite a rebel. He is the organizer of a private tempest in a teapot. He is invariable in his individualism; his rebellions take place, not within a political party, but in splendid isolation . . . Out of inner necessity, therefore, he becomes a specialist in reducing bourgeois values to absurdity, because all who hold such values are a source of inner reproach to him.

EDMUND BERGLER
The Psychology of Gambling (1958)

———•◆•———

I've always been asked what it takes to be a professional poker player. Well, you must have a strong constitution and no nerves whatsoever. And you have to be an honest man. All the stock in trade that a gambler has is his word . . . In a room full of professional gamblers, we can walk off and leave all our chips on the table . . . Now, go play in some of those private games with some of these goody two-shoes, and see how you come out if you leave your pile unattended for a minute.

"AMARILLO SLIM" PRESTON
with Bill G. Cox
Play Poker to Win (1973)

Christ, he thin. Look at him. He looks like the advance man for a famine.

Sarge on Amarillo Slim
quoted in Jon Bradshaw, *Fast Company* (1975)

———— •◆• ————

A gambler's word is his bond. If one these boys tells you a goose'll move a plow, then hook him up, neighbor.

Johnny Moss, world-champion poker player
quoted in Jon Bradshaw, *Fast Company* (1975)

———— •◆• ————

Gamblers, with but few exceptions, are the most honest men in the world.

Nick "The Greek" Dandalos
quoted in Cy Rice, *Nick the Greek: King of Gamblers* (1969)

———— •◆• ————

Gamblers are the most broadminded people in the world. If more folks were like 'em, there would be fewer laws.

Pug Pearson
quoted in Jon Bradshaw, *Fast Company* (1975)

The lowest pool hustler in the business is four times more respectable than some of those humbugs in Washington.

> MINNESOTA FATS
> quoted in Jon Bradshaw, *Fast Company* (1975)

———— • ◆ • ————

Once, when I agreed to do a television commercial for Edge shaving cream, a New York ad agency sent me the story-boards, which called for me to say, "for a smoother shave, it's Edge, three-to-one." They included the results of a poll from which the figures were taken. I checked them, and it came to five to two. I told the account man that the commercial had to be changed.

> JIMMY "THE GREEK" SNYDER
> *Jimmy the Greek, by Himself* (1975)
> with Mickey Herskowitz and Steve Perkins

———— • ◆ • ————

At the card game, one of the boys looked across the table and said, "Now Reuben, play the cards fair. I know what I dealt you."

> LYNDON B. JOHNSON
> quoted in Mike Caro, *Mike Caro's Book of Tells* (1984)

What was I supposed to do, call him for cheating better than me in front of the others?

DOYLE LONNIGAN
after being outcheated by Henry Gondorf
in David S. Ward (screenwriter)
The Sting (1973)

———◆———

Though at the beginning the table was half covered with gold, yet before the play ended . . . there was scarce a single guinea to be seen on the table; and this was the stranger as every person present, except myself, declared he had lost; and what was become of the money, unless the devil himself carried it away, is difficult to determine.

HENRY FIELDING
Tom Jones (1749)

———◆———

They live without laws and yet obey the laws of the dice . . . When the unsuccessful gamester has lost his all, he sets his liberty, and even his life, upon a single cast, and is accounted infamous if he does not pay his debts of honour.

ST. AMBROSE (A.D. 397)
on "the Huns"

What is gamesmanship? Most difficult of questions to answer briefly. "The Art of Winning Games Without Actually Cheating"—that is my personal definition.

STEPHAN POTTER
Gamesmanship: The Art of Winning without Actually Cheating (1962)

———— • ◆ • ————

One might ask why gambling debts are so rigorously honored in polite society while the same people often feel little scruple in neglecting far more sacred debts. The answer lies in the fact that in gambling one accepts a man's word in a situation where there is no legal recourse. A trust has been extended to which one must respond.

DENIS DIDEROT AND JEAN D'ALEMBERT
L'encyclopidie (1757)

———— • ◆ • ————

People don't understand that the gambler may be the most virtuous of men. I know a man who habitually cheats at cards, but he will give his last penny to a beggar. And at the same time he will never miss a chance to get into a game where a sucker is to be trimmed.

NIKOLAI GOGOL
The Gamblers (1842)
translated by Alexander Berkman

MACON: You just about cleaned everybody, fella—I don't think you lost since you got the deal . . . What's the secret of your success?

MUSTACHED MAN: Prayer.

> WILLIAM GOLDMAN (SCREENWRITER)
> *Butch Cassidy and the Sundance Kid* (1969)

———•◆•———

PLAYED FIVE ACES

NOW PLAYING A HARP

> CHEATER'S TOMBSTONE

———•◆•———

How they will go about, if they perceive an honest man have moneye, which list not playe, to provoke him to playe! . . . Now all of this is to make him to beginne, for they knowe if he be once in, and be a loser, that he will not sticke at his twelve-pence, but hopeth ever to get it againe, whiles perhappes he will lose all.

> ROGER ASCHAM (1515–68)
> tutor of Queen Elizabeth
> quoted in John Ashton, *The History of Gambling in England* (1898)

I never, ever shot more than a stroke or two better'n the opposition. If a man shoots eight-nine, I shoot eight-eight. If a man shoots sixty-eight, I shoot sixty-seven. I never liked to add insult to injury.

TITANIC THOMPSON
quoted in Jon Bradshaw, *Fast Company* (1975)

I understood the game well enough, though I pretended I did not.

DANIEL DEFOE
Moll Flanders (1722)

He justly suspected that they had concealed their skill, with a view of stripping him on some other occasion; for he could not suppose, that persons of their figure and character, should be, in reality, such novices as they affected to appear.

TOBIAS SMOLLETT
The Adventure of Ferdinand Count Fathom (1753)

When a poker game started it was discovered that there were no chips, a rare omission on a river steamboat. The boat had a cargo of corn, so it was decided to shell some and use the kernels for chips. In a little while the stranger slipped away and managed to get into the dark hold where the corn was stowed. He hastily shelled an ear and put the kernels in his coat pocket. He then entered the game . . . All may have been well, except that the ear of corn he shelled in the dark was red! Nobody knew for certain what happened to him, but one report said he was bound hand and foot and carried off the boat by the other players.

> ALLEN DOWLING
> *The Great American Pastime* (1970)

A clothing store clerk here found himself put to a strange use in a poolroom recently. He was a newcomer and got fresh with declaring himself to the natives. "What can we do with him," inquired one poolroom lounger of another after taking the stranger's measure. "Chalk his head and use him for a cue" was the response. The suggestion was literally carried out. The pool balls were pyramided in the center of the table and the cue ball was propelled by punching it with the clothing store clerk's head.

> *ILLUSTRATED POLICE NEWS* (1887)
> quoted in John Grissim, *Billiards* (1979)

A gambler without an excuse is a gambler who can't continue.

CHARLES BUKOWSKI (1920–94)

———•◆•———

It is much nicer to hustle three-cushion instead of pool, because you rob a more refined type of person. In three-cushion, the worst that can happen is to have the guy ask you if you will take a check.

DAN MCGOORTY
as told to Robert Byrne, *McGoorty* (1972)

———•◆•———

Some of those hustlers are fabulous liars, really fabulous, when it comes to talkin' about who they beat and for how much cash. It's a congenital disease. Some of them guys would derange a lie detector, drive it stark raving mad.

MINNESOTA FATS
quoted in Jon Bradshaw, *Fast Company* (1975)

———•◆•———

The easiest people to con . . . are con men.

MARTY REISMAN
The Money Player (1974)

You see players today whipping out a handkerchief just when the man at the table is about to shoot, but you should have seen the way Alfredo did it. It was masterful. He kept his hand-kerchief folded like an accordion, with the tip sticking out so he could grab it without fumbling . . . When he snaked it out of his pocket he always sort of shook it to the right and left like a long scarf before putting it to his nose and honking.

> Dan McGoorty
> on Alfredo De Oro
> as told to Robert Byrne, *McGoorty* (1972)

———— • ◆ • ————

Fishing and poker are analogous: one has to become quite good at either to realize that, in comparing one man's "take" with another's, the element of luck is almost nonexistent; the expert nearly always gets more. There are times when even the best bass angler cannot discover bass that are feeding, and times when even the slickest professional gambler cannot find his suckers. But there is hardly a day when the real adept at either cannot at least do well enough for eating purposes.

> Jason Lucas
> quoted in A. D. Livingston, *Poker Strategy and Winning Play*
> (1971)

He compared gambling to a trout fisherman catching fish, not for eating purposes, but merely for the thrill of the catch.

CY RICE
Nick the Greek: King of Gamblers (1969)

———•◆•———

"Man, you got the pure art. But you're going to need more than that if you sit down with Lancey Hodges. He's a dead eye, no nerves at all, and steel-minded, and Kid, *he knows*."

RICHARD JESSUP
The Cincinnati Kid (1963)

———•◆•———

I've got nothing against them playing, but those big hand-bags they keep on their laps worry me. The bags are always about to fall, and they grab them just in time; and when they're not keeping the bags from falling they're digging into them, and you don't know if they're coming up with lipstick, ciagrettes, an automatic, or a spare ace!

AN OLD-TIMER ON WOMEN POKER PLAYERS
quoted in Allen Dowling, *The Great American Pastime* (1970)

Men who are playing poker tend to be pretty macho . . . They can't stand to be beaten by you, so they overplay their hands, they put too many bets in, they raise you too often, and they won't fold against you.

> ANNIE DUKE
> quoted in Adam Platt, "Women Are Beating the Pants Off Men in the Macho World of High-Stakes Poker," *Elle* (1996)

———•◆•———

The male ego has an irritating habit of suspending natural poker instincts.

> ANTHONY HOLDEN
> *Big Deal* (1990)

———•◆•———

At my age I suppose I should be knitting. I would rather play poker with five or six experts.

> POKER ALICE
> quoted in Nolie Mumey, *Poker Alice* (1951)

He attracted people like fish to a flashpan, people who begged him to play with their money. It was the legend and the charm and, no doubt, the idea of sharing winnings with Nick the Greek. He was beautiful with women. He made Omar Sharif look like a truck driver.

> JIMMY "THE GREEK" SNYDER ON NICK "THE GREEK" DANDALOS
> quoted in *Jimmy the Greek, by Himself* (1975)
> with Mickey Herskowitz and Steve Perkins

———◆———

We needed money real bad at home and my daddy told me I had to stop work or stop gamblin'. And I said, "Daddy, if I don't work how can I get money to gamble?" And Daddy, he said, "Son, that's what gamblers got to figure out." So I quit work.

> JOHNNY MOSS, WORLD-CHAMPION POKER PLAYER
> quoted in Jon Bradshaw, *Fast Company* (1975)

———◆———

I hustled for cokes and change, and if they had some that folded and some nerve, I would unfold it for them. I started in there when I was 13 and when I was 14 I got my stroke. I got my stroke and learned to count. I beat every kid in the Y and then I started lookin' around. I just kept looking.

> JERSEY RED
> quoted in Ned Polsky, *Hustlers, Beats, and Others* (1998)

There's a sucker born every minute.

PHINEAS T. BARNUM (1810–91)

The phrase [sucker] is sometimes applied in billiard saloons
to persons of the same genus to which it is applied elsewhere.

MICHAEL PHELAN
The Game of Billiards (1857)

And remember, Dearie, never give a sucker an even break.

W. C. FIELDS
Poppy (1936)

A sucker has to die every minute to make room for the one
that is born.

POLICE GAZETTE (1907)
quoted in Herbert Asbury, *Sucker's Progress* (1938)

And studied each fresh sucker with a practiced eye . . .
Frankie would sit back wearily, sick of seeing them come on
begging to be hustled, wondering where in the world they all
came from . . . and why in the world they always, always,
always came back for more.

NELSON ALGREN
The Man with the Golden Arm (1949)

In a bet there is a fool and a thief.

PROVERB

"You tricked yourself, simpleton."

HERBERT O. YARDLEY
The Education of a Poker Player (1957)

"I hope I break even tonight," was the sucker's philosophy. "I
need the money so bad."

NELSON ALGREN
The Man with the Golden Arm (1949)

Only the existentially terrified *play* to break even. Aren't we after what dailiness seldom provides?

STEPHEN DUNN
"Gambling: Remembrances and Assertions" (1993)

————•◆•————

It is the *greed* of the sucker that makes the hustler's skill pay.

DAVID SPANIER
Total Poker (1977)

————•◆•————

"You can shear a sheep many times, but you can only skin him once."

AMARILLO SLIM
quoted in Anthony Holden, *Big Deal* (1990)

————•◆•————

"Sometimes the lambs slaughter the butcher."

AMARILLO SLIM
quoted in in Anthony Holden, *Big Deal* (1990)

Those spunging Caterpillars which swarm where any Billiard-Tables are set up, for this is where they wait for ignorant Cullies to be their Customers.

CHARLES COTTON
The Compleate Gamester (1674)

———————◆———————

Suckers must be stomped for their love of ignorance, for expecting too much from life. Suckers do not realize that a man like Billy spent six hours a day at pool tables all over Albany for years learning how to shed his ignorance.

WILLIAM KENNEDY
Billy Phelan's Greatest Game (1978)

———————◆———————

She played unevenly, as if chance was all she had. She reeled them in. The game went on. The dog was stiff now, poised on Lily's knees, a ball of vicious muscle with its yellow eyes slit in concentration. It gave advice, seemed to sniff the lay of Fleur's cards, twitched and nudged.

LOUISE ERDRICH
"Fleur" (1986)

The onlookers, who had placed bets on the players, were even more passionate than those who were playing . . . It got so tense that when the onlookers said anything they were pounced upon.

BEN OKRI
The Famished Road (1991)

———◆———

A railbird is a busted card player standing on the rail.

REX JONES
The Railbird (1984)

———◆———

There is even greater danger to be found in kibbitzers, if they favor your opponent.

GEROLAMO CARDANO
The Book on Games of Chance (c. 1520)

———◆———

The side-betting . . . consists then in a rising crescendo of shouts.

CLIFFORD GEERTZ
"Deep Play: Notes on the Balinese Cockfight" (1972)

Never had I shared so intimately in any game in which I myself had been a player, as I shared now in the reflexion of this stranger's excitement.

STEPHAN ZWEIG
Four-and-Twenty Hours in a Woman's Life (1926)
translated by Eden and Cedar Paul

———◆———

The type of gambler that hangs around the tables holding on to his room rent. Can't bear to leave, but can't lay it on the table either.

JACK RICHARDSON
Xmas in Las Vegas (1962)

———◆———

Where there's money there are people who, if you give them some of the money, will tell you what to do with the rest of it. In the stock market they are called analysts . . . brokers. In sports they are called handicappers.

LARRY MERCHANT
The National Football Lottery (1973)

Before he turned thirty he had twice staked virtually all his possessions on gambling events, and in 1805 he killed a man, and nearly died himself, in a duel fought to settle an argument issuing from the terms of a bet on a horse race.

> JOHN M. FINDLAY
> on Andrew Jackson
> *People of Chance: Gambling in American Society from Jamestown to Las Vegas* (1986)

At home all day playing cards.

> GEORGE WASHINGTON
> *Diary* (September 5, 1770)

Marie Antoinette owned a cue made of a single piece of ivory. She reportedly valued it so much that she wore the key to the cabinet in which it was stored around her neck.

> MIKE SHAMOS
> *Pool: History, Strategies, and Legends* (1994)

Sitting by the table, I noticed that Wild Bill Hickok seemed sleeply and inattentive. So I kept a close watch on the other fellow. Presently I observed that one of his opponents was occasionally dropping a card in his hat, which he held in his lap, until a number of cards had been laid away for future use in the game. The pot had gone around several times and was steadily raised by some of the players, Bill staying right alone, though he still seemed to be drowsy. The bets kept rising. At last the man with the hat full of cards picked a hand out of his reserves, put the hat on his head, and raised Bill two hundred dollars. Bill came back with a raise of two hundred, and as the other covered it he quietly shoved a pistol into his face and observed, "I'm calling the hand that's in your hat."

BUFFALO BILL CODY (1876)
rounded up by Greg Stebbin and Terry Hall, *Cowboy Wisdom* (1995)

When Hickok was in danger of being cleaned out by a pair of crooked poker sharks, he called the largest raise of the evening with his last greenbacks. At the showdown, one of his opponents displayed the winning hand and Bill tossed in his cards. "Hold it!" he said, as the sharper reached for the pot. Drawing two revolvers, he leveled them at the swindlers. "I have a pair of sixes, and they beat anything."

ROBERT K. DEARMENT
Knights of the Green Cloth: The Saga of the Frontier Gamblers
(1892)

11

The Capital of Chance and Other Shrines

There are no clocks in the palace of pleasure.

FLORENTINE PROVERB

Creation's okay. But if God'd had money, he'd have done this.

STEVE WYNN
on Las Vegas
quoted in Anthony Holden,
Big Deal (1990)

The main nerve of the American Dream.

HUNTER THOMPSON
on Las Vegas
Fear and Loathing in Las Vegas (1971)

An "A" place has action, alcohol, and other farewells to the cares and responsibilities of the workaday world. "A" places offer excitement, thrill, permission, the prospect of quick gain, and the company of others who seek the same. Unlike football, basketball, or soccer, gambling games generally have no time periods or clearly defined endpoints. For the time allotted you can voluntarily lose yourself, in cards, dice, calculation, conversation, and if you're not careful you can lose your socks. Truth is, if you don't have much allotted time you might want to avoid "A" places, because when you get there your watch tends to move at a different speed, and you may have to call a bus station for the time, since there may not be working clocks in the house. If there are, as Anthony Holden puts it, you may be "stupendously innocent about the A.M. or P.M. dimensions to the hour on display." Quite a few gamblers I know have had even more drastic experiences like that of the poker player Pug Pearson, who describes how he "got up from a table once, turned around a couple of times, and five or six years had gone by." By that point you run the risk that your "A" place will lose its shimmer and become more like home than a place of fugitive excesses that makes your heart hop-skip on approach.

This section includes descriptions of several "A" places, but spotlights Las Vegas, which has undoubtedly been the mecca of "A" places for most gamble-minded Americans since gangster Bugsy Siegel opened the first hotel, choosing

Abbott and Costello for the opening act, and the likes of John F. Kennedy started partying there with the likes of Frank Sinatra. In Spanish this distinctly indoor-oriented town means "the meadows," and though in money terms it often means Loss Vegas, for most visitors, Lost Wages or not, it translates into a stimulating time.

With its pervasive Old West themes—a strip called Glitter Gulch, hotels with names like the Golden Nugget, chintzy neon pioneer wagons, and a city motto of "Still a Frontier Town"—Las Vegas self-consciously illuminates a national nostalgia for a time of gamble, when immigrants and prospectors took their chances for a better life. The spectacular and continued growth of Las Vegas—and the explosion of casino gambling throughout the country—suggests that the *A* in "A" places might be taken for an aspect of America as well.

After flying over hundreds of miles of brown, barren nothingness, all of a sudden there's a sparkle and excitement in the atmosphere: you're approaching Las Vegas! The air feels different. It's narcotic.

DAVID A. DANIEL
Poker: How to Win at the Great American Game (1997)

————•◆•————

You know you've arrived in Las Vegas while your insides are still on the plane.

ANTHONY HOLDEN
Big Deal (1990)

————•◆•————

I have stepped out onto the Las Vegas strip with a smile on my face that you couldn't have wiped off with a shovel.

EDWARD ALLEN
"Penny Ante" (1992)

————•◆•————

When we enter a casino, the whole world undergoes a major change.

MIRON STABINSKY WITH JEREMY SILMAN
Zen and the Art of Casino Gambling (1995)

The City of Fish and Chips: Some poor fish is always losing his chips.

> HOD SHEWELL
> quoted in Lance Humble, Ph.D., and Carl Cooper, Ph.D.,
> *The World's Greatest Blackjack Book* (1980)

———•◆•———

On a three-day visit to Vegas you can have one of the best times of your life. To do that you have to forget about great museums, the pleasure of reading, great theater, great music, stimulating lectures by great philosophers, great food, great wine, and true love. Forget about them.

> MARIO PUZO
> *Inside Las Vegas* (1976)

———•◆•———

The relatively undiminished activity of pre-dawn Las Vegas raises her spirits.

> JOHN O'BRIEN
> *Leaving Las Vegas* (1990)

———•◆•———

[Vegas] looks like somebody took one of Liberace's jackets and made a city out of it.

> LANCE HUMBLE, PH.D., AND CARL COOPER, PH.D.
> *The World's Greatest Blackjack Book* (1980)

Las Vegas is the only town in the world whose skyline is made up neither of buildings, like New York, nor of trees, like Wilbraham, Massachusetts, but signs.

TOM WOLFE
The Kandy-Kolored Tangerine-Flake Streamline Baby (1965)

———— •◆• ————

"Vegas runs on juice. You sometimes here someone say, 'I've got more juice than Minute Maid.' That means he's got friends."

MARVIN BERLIN
quoted in John Gregory Dunne, *Vegas: A Memoir of a Dark Season* (1974)

———— •◆• ————

People in the rest of the world merely go broke and die broke. In Vegas, you live broke.

SHERLOCK FELDMAN
quoted in Edward Reid and Ovid Demaris, *The Green Felt Jungle* (1965)

———— •◆• ————

From all my reading of the history of gambling from the beginning of civilization to the present, I must say that the present-day Vegas gambling is the most regulated and most honest that has ever existed.

MARIO PUZO
Inside Las Vegas (1976)

The only way to double your money in Las Vegas is to fold it in half and put it back in your pocket.

> NIPSEY RUSSELL, COMEDIAN
> quoted in Arthur S. Reber, *The New Gambler's Bible* (1996)

———— •◆• ————

It has nothing for export but its promise. Its growth was not only conspicuous, conspicuous was the only medium of its growth.

> MICHAEL HERR
> *The Big Room* (1986)

———— •◆• ————

When I walked into the Mirage Hotel's Race and Sports Book to begin a week of all-out gambling and gazed at the giant television screens and electronic displays on the wall, I wondered if I had died and gone to a horseplayer's heaven.

> ANDREW BEYER
> *Beyer on Speed* (1993)

———— •◆• ————

When I came to Las Vegas for the first time and heard the siren sounds of dice and cards on green felt tables, I experienced odd and almost incredible sensations of invincibility; given luck and self-control, I, too, might make my fortune here.

> JON BRADSHAW
> *Fast Company* (1975)

You may have heard about the tourist vacationing in Las Vegas. He didn't have any money to gamble, so he just watched the games and bet mentally. In no time at all, he'd lost his mind.

HOLLY SHAW
quoted in Lance Humble, Ph.D., and Carl Cooper, Ph.D., *The World's Greatest Blackjack Book* (1980)

———•◆•———

Some place in the richest nation in the world, there has to be a city with no other excuse for being than money.

WILLIAM SAROYAN
quoted in John M. Findlay, *People of Chance* (1986)

———•◆•———

"Las Vegas is like a parasite that feeds on money," said a man from Texas. "It sits here in the middle of the desert and produces absolutely nothing, yet it supports a half a million people . . . I guess it's a kind of modern miracle, something like loaves and fishes."

ALVIN ALVAREZ
The Biggest Game in Town (1983)

. . . so you're down on the main floor playing blackjack, and the stakes are getting high when suddenly you chance to look up, and there, right smack above you is a half-naked fourteen-year-old girl being chased through the air by a snarling wolverine . . . the gambling action runs twenty-four hours a day on the main floor, and the circus never ends.

> HUNTER THOMPSON
> *Fear and Loathing in Las Vegas* (1971)

I entered the casino with such firm confidence, yet, at the same time, in a state of such excitement as I had never experienced before.

> FYODOR DOSTOEVSKY
> *The Gambler* (1867)
> translated by Victor Terras

Even as I approach the gambling hall, as soon as I hear, still two rooms away, the jingle of money poured out on the table, I almost go into convulsions.

> FYODOR DOSTOEVSKY
> *The Gambler* (1867)
> translated by Victor Terras

People are supposed to gamble here, people are supposed to drink here, people are supposed to spend their days here in pursuit of skill, cunning, comradeship, and money. No one is supposed to be pompous here, or intrusive, or boring; no one will be held accountable for the bets they make, or the way that they comfort themselves. But if they choose, they can choose to be left alone.

DAVID MAMET
"Pool Halls" (1986)

———•◆•———

There was a strange, almost reverential silence about the place. In the far corner of the room, barely visible beyond a periphery of light, a gallery of ancient men watched a one-pocket game through the haze of blue smoke, their hushed concentration marred only by the soft click of the balls, a stool being moved or the squeak of the cue tip as it took the chalk.

JOHN GRISSIM
Billiards (1979)

As I leaned on the clubroom railing . . . and looked for the first time at the Gardena players the notion struck me that the inhabitants of this room had been shuffling, cutting and squeezing their cards not for 60 hours, or even for 60 years, but forever—as though in some prehistoric age they had been quick-frozen and tucked into a time capsule until, thawed by the California sun, they resumed their play heedless of the interruption.

DICK MILES
"Lowball in a Time Capsule" (1970)

When I was young, the poolroom where I lived was very old. By the summer of 1969, when the road player walked into that elegantly dissipated atmosphere of stale beer, stale cigar smoke, and the stale aspirations of old men, past the big front window where sallow, rebellious eighth-graders slouched, eating Slim Jims and Planters peanuts, smirking nervously at the good people who walked by on Illinois Avenue and hoping none of them were their mothers.

DAVID McCUMBER
Off the Rail (1996)

It is a very dirty room over the garage, and full of smoke, and the crap game is on an old pool table; and around the table and packed in so close you cannot get a knitting needle between any two guys with a mawl, are all the high shots in town, for there is plenty of money around at this time, and many citizens are very prosperous. Furthermore, I wish to say there are some very tough guys around the table, too, including guys who will shoot you in the head, or maybe the stomach, and think nothing whatever about the matter.

DAMON RUNYON
"Blood Pressure" (1929)

———— •◆• ————

Out of the seven saloons which ran poker games, Monty's Place was the only clean one. The poker room itself was at the rear of the saloon and was about twenty feet square with two barred windows high above the ground and an iron wood stove at the end kept polished by the town idiot, called Dummy.

HERBERT O. YARDLEY
The Education of a Poker Player (1957)

No gaming in the eating room, except tossing up for reckonings, on penalty of paying the whole bill of the members present.

RULE NO. 21 OF THE ALMACK CLUB (FOUNDED 1764)
quoted in John Ashton, *History of Gambling in England* (1898)

———— •◆• ————

There was a time in this country when men could be found who would bet their eyeballs out and yours too, on what they believed to be an even thing, but that was before barbering came into vogue. Now our big operators want a flash at your hole card before loosening up.

W. B. "BAT" MASTERSON
New York Morning Telegraph (1921)

———— •◆• ————

I come from a dizzy land where the lottery is the basis of reality.

JORGE LUIS BORGES
"The Lottery in Babylon" (1957)

"You gotta walk around carrying their vig on your back like some sort of coolie. Everyone's supposed to be equal in this country, so how come the house gets a five percent edge?"

"That's the entertainment tax," I answered.

JACK RICHARDSON
Memoir of a Gambler (1979)

———•◆•———

At Monte Carlo there is still the plush mustiness of the 19th century noble lions—of Baron Bleichroden, a big winner at roulette . . . Of Lord Jersey, who won seventeen maximum bets in a row . . . nodded to the croupier, and said, "Much obliged, old sport, old sport," took his winnings to England, retired to the country and never gambled again in his life.

TOM WOLFE
The Kandy-Kolored Tangerine-Flake Streamline Baby (1965)

It was a sparkling scene. There were perhaps fifty men in the room, the majority in dinner jackets, all at ease with themselves and their surroundings, all stimulated by . . . the prospect of high gambling, the grand slam, the ace pot, the key-throw in a 64 game of backgammon . . . the elegance of the room invested each with a kind of aristocracy.

> IAN FLEMING
> *Moonraker* (1955)

———•◆•———

Monte Carlo has the right idea; fix a game where you are going to get people's money, but the people don't mind you getting it. A fellow can always get over losing money in a game of chance, but he seems so constituted that he can never get over money thrown away to a government in taxes.

> WILL ROGERS
> "A Visit to Monte Carlo"
> *A Will Rogers Treasury* (1982)

He was beginning to get the feel of Atlantic City and its sur-rounding geography and was getting to like it. At least it amazed him, held his attention, to see an old seaside resort being done over in Las Vegas plastic, given that speedline look . . . Here you are in wonderland, it told the working people getting off the tour busses, all these serious faces coming to have a good time.

ELMORE LEONARD
Glitz (1985)

On the Boardwalk in Atlantic City,
Life will be Peaches and Cream.

OLD SONG

12

All In

Big, Bad, and Beautiful Bets

Under the influence of uncontrollable ecstasy the players
gambled their wives, their children and ultimately themselves
into captivity.

TACITUS
Germanicus (A.D. 99)

Sugar Ray [Robinson] wanted to challenge me in golf and
boxing using a handicap system. In golf, he wanted me to give
him a stroke a hole, which I think I could have handled, but
what he proposed in boxing didn't fit my instinct as a gambler.
He said he'd spot me five rounds in a six-round fight. I said,
"That's fine, as long as I can use my wedge."

SAM SNEAD WITH FRAN PIROZZOLO
The Game I Love (1997)

You name it, someone, somewhere has bet on it.

And no matter how extravagant the wager, someone has staked it. Next to the Indian ruler Yudihishthira, for instance, today's high-rolling "whales" look like penny-pitching potzers. Yudihishthira bet a hundred thousand slaves on a roll of the dice, he bet his kingdom, himself, and finally he bet his wife, Draupedi. Draupedi quite logically pointed out that since he had lost himself first he wasn't in a position to wager her.

This section contains a smorgasbord of wagers indicative of the shapes gamble takes, from the comedic that sustains us flawed humanoids to the aggressive gamble that threatens destruction (the Bay of Pigs has been described as "one hell of a gamble"). For my money, the closest to the play spirit of gamble, and the most entertaining, are those wagers of the spontaneous can-do proposition-bet variety:

> "I'd gladly bet a thousand pounds that a journey like that, made under those conditions, is impossible."
> "On the contrary, it's quite possible," Fogg replied.
>
> JULES VERNE
> *Around the World in Eighty Days* (1873)

Emerging out of casual conversation (here over a game of whist), this sort of bet has a life, wit, and etiquette of its own that follows a general structure. It begins in a simple equation:

I can + You can't = a bet

I can go around the world in eighty days. I can jump a motor-cyle over X. Listen:

> LUKE: I can eat fifty eggs.
> DRAGLINE: Nobody kin eat fifty eggs . . . (to Luke) You ever eat fifty eggs?
> LUKE: Nobody ever ate fifty eggs.
> GAMBLER: Bet! Bet! Babalugats!
> DRAGLINE: Mah boy say he kin eat fifty eggs, he'll eat fifty eggs.
> LOUDMOUTH STEVE: Yeah but in how long?
> LUKE: One hour.

Conditions of the bet must be clarified because failure to do so can give losers an excuse to welch or pick a bone, though the moment after the original statement is generally one moment too late to renegotiate the opening proposition.

> DRAGLINE: Why'd you have to say fifty? Why not thirty-five or thirty-nine?
> LUKE: Seems like a nice round number.
> DRAGLINE: Luke, that's money you're talking about. What's the matter with you?
> LUKE: Yeah, well, it's somethin' to do.
>
> FRANK R. PIERSON AND HAL DRESNER (SCREENWRITERS)
> *Cool Hand Luke* (1967)

Bon appétit!

It is quite certain that no two human beings can be anywhere without ere long offering to "bet" upon something.

ANDREW STEINMETZ
The Gaming Table (1870)

———•◆•———

In England a working man was arrested for hanging another man. The man being hanged defended his hanger. He'd lost a bet and the stakes were that the winner could hang the loser. They had to bet something and all they had to bet was their lives.

MARIO PUZO
Inside Las Vegas (1976)

———•◆•———

From China in the fourth century B.C. comes a poem telling the story of two gamblers who, having nothing else to stake, bet their ears on which side of a birch leaf would lie uppermost after its fall from the tree; the loser honorably severed the lobes of his ears and presented them on the leaf to the winner.

ALAN WYKES
The Complete Illustrated Guide to Gambling (1964)

Once a wager was made, there was no acceptable excuse for withdrawing it. The race could be canceled only if one of the horses died between the date of the wager and the time set for the contest. These strict rules are illustrated in a breach of contract suit tried in Henrico in August, 1690. Gentlemen of the highest dignity and reputation appeared as witnesses, and the case illustrates, too, the high standing of racing in colonial society.

JANE CARSON
Colonial Virginians at Play (1965)

———•◆•———

Gambling obsessed men and women, rich or poor. Raindrops running down a window pane, the fertility of a dean's wife, steeplechasing by moonlight, anything and everything were grounds for a bet.

J. H. PLUMB
The First Four Georges (1956)

Of all the high players this country ever sees, there is no doubt that the guy they call The Sky is the highest. He will bet all he has, and nobody can bet more than this. The Sky is a great hand for propositions, such as are always coming up among citizens who follow games of chance for a living. And no one ever sees The Sky when he does not have some proposition of his own.

DAMON RUNYON
"The Idyll of Miss Sarah Brown" (1947)

The biggest and first crap game is mentioned in Greek mythology. Zeus, Poseidon, and Hades rolled dice for shares of the Universe. Poseidon won the Oceans. Hades won the Underworld. Zeus won the Heavens and is suspected of having used loaded dice.

MARIO PUZO
Inside Las Vegas (1976)

You may read, in our histories, how Sir Miles Partridge played at Dice with King Henry the Eighth for Jesus Bells, so called, which were the greatest in England, and hung in a tower of St. Paul's Church; and won them; whereby he brought them to ring in his pocket; but the ropes, afterwards, catched about his neck, for, in Edward the Sixth's days, he was hanged for some criminal offences.

JOHN ASHTON
The History of Gambling in England (1898)

———— • ◆ • ————

This began as a cattleman's game, became an oilman's game, and now it's the kind of game only South American dictators in exile can afford to be in. Now, neighbor, that's real high poker.

AMARILLO SLIM
quoted in Jon Bradshaw, *Fast Company* (1975)

His Heaviness said he could out-eat anybody and often won big bets proving it. One spiel involved a challenger named (what else?) Tiny, a giant of a man who had to be brought to the restaurant on a flatbed truck. While waiting for the contest to begin, Wanderone warmed up by eating a leg of lamb. Tiny was so big his backers "couldn't get him into the joint until they smeared chicken fat on the door."

ROBERT BYRNE
on Minnesota Fats
Byrne's Wonderful World of Pool and Billiards (1996)

———— ◆ ————

Now-a-days, not content with carrying his purse to the gaming table, the gamester conveys his iron chest to the playroom. It is there that, as soon as the gaming instruments are distributed, you witness the most terrible contests.

JUVENAL
Satires (127–100 B.C.)

I hereby challenge to fight any man in the country of 44 years of age and 12st., and my wife shall fight any woman in the country, bar none; and my dog shall fight any dog in the country 48 lbs.; and my cock shall fight any cock in the county of any weight; each battle shall be for five pounds a side.

> JOSEPH HILTON
> challenge issued to any "Man, Woman, Dog and Cock" (1845)
> quoted in Peter Charlton, *Two Flies Up a Wall: The Australian Passion for Gambling* (1987)

If you can make one heap
　of all your winnings,
And risk it on one turn of
　pitch-and-toss
And lose and start again
　at your beginnings . . .
Then you're a man, my son.

> RUDYARD KIPLING
> "If" (1910)

He'll bet on anything that moves. Christ, he'd bet on a *cockroach* race.

> PUG PEARSON
> on Jack "Treetop" Strauss
> quoted in Jon Bradshaw, *Fast Company* (1975)

———•◆•———

The hand of Fate and a hand of poker combined to give him the plantation which he afterwards called Tara . . . such was his faith in his destiny and four deuces that he never for a moment wondered just how the money would be paid back should a higher hand be laid across the table.

> MARGARET MITCHELL
> *Gone with the Wind* (1936)

———•◆•———

The Russians were bluffing. They didn't want a world war over Cuba. We had all the cards in our hands; there was no way they could win. Of course you might say that the U.S. was bluffing too, because we didn't want a world war either. But we were bluffing with the best hand.

> GENERAL DAVID SHROUP
> quoted in David Halberstam, *The Best and the Brightest* (1972)

At this game they hazard all they possess, and many do not leave till they are almost stripped quite naked and till they have lost all they have in their cabins. Some have been known to stake their liberty for a time, which fully proves their passion for this game, for there are no men in the world more jealous of their liberty than the savages.

PIERRE FRANÇOIS XAVIER DE CHARLEVOIX
on Huron dice-playing (1744)

Gates and another millionaire, John Drake, often used to meet for dinner at a Chicago hotel. One of their favorite pastimes was moistening two lumps of sugar and counting the number of times a fly landed on each lump. The man whose sugar lump attracted the most flies not only won the game, but collected an extra $1000 for each landing he won by.

ALICE FLEMING
Something for Nothing: A History of Gambling (1978)

John W. "Bet-a-Million" Gates, the barbed-wire king, who in 1897 on a train between Chicago and Pittsburg, apparently won $22,000 by betting on raindrop races, a window pane serving as a course.

HERBERT ASBURY
Sucker's Progress (1938)

———•◆•———

If he lost his wife upbraided him, and . . . he bought her silence and her favours by showering her with diamonds and costly gifts. If he came home a winner she used to tie on an apron and make flapjacks for him on the stove in their luxury suite.

L. J. LUDOVICI
on John "Bet-a-Million" Gates
The Itch for Play (1962)

———•◆•———

An unhappy boy that kept his father's sheepe in the country, did use to carry a paire of Cards in his pocket, and, meeting with boyes as good as himselfe, would fall to cards at the Cambrian game of whip-her-ginny, or English One and Thirty; at which sport, hee would some dayes lose a sheepe or two.

EDWARD TAYLOR
Wit and Mirth

Inman himself had lost an entire cow . . . He had bet it away piece by piece, point by point. Saying in the heat of play, I'll wager the tenderloin of that heifer on the next point. Or, Every rip on the left of my betting cow says we win. As the two camps parted ways, Inman's heifer was still walking, but various Cherokee had claim to its many partitions.

CHARLES FRAZIER
Cold Mountain (1997)

Once I lost ten blue chips to a player who bet me that the pale light we happened to notice filtering through the curtains was dusk, not dawn.

DICK MILES
"Lowball in a Time Capsule" (1970)

Has there ever been a dramatic movie or TV sequence when the final bet was modest?

ALLEN DOWLING
The Great American Pastime (1970)

Many stories are told of the fabulous high stakes games, the best known probably being of the flashy, big time gambler who sat in a game with a group of Texas oil moguls. Wishing to let them know immediately that with him money was no object, he grandly came forth with a roll of ten thousand dollars and called for a stack of chips. The banker promptly accommodated him—with one white chip, an ante.

ALLEN DOWLING
The Great American Pastime (1970)

———•◆•———

I have set my life upon a cast,
And I will stand the hazard of the die.

WILLIAM SHAKESPEARE
Richard II (1596)

———•◆•———

They have put in the papers a good story made on White's; a man dropped down dead at the door, was carried in; the club immediately made bets whether he was dead or not, and when they were going to bleed him, the wagerers for death interposed, and said it would affect the fairness of the bet.

HORACE WALPOLE
letter to Horace Mann (1750)

"You say . . . if I make this lighter light ten times running I win a Cadillac. If it misses just once then I forfeit the little finger of my left hand. Is that right?"

"Don't you think this is rather a silly bet?" I said.

"I think it's a fine bet," the boy answered.

"I think it's a stupid, ridiculous bet," the girl said. "What'll happen if you lose?"

"It won't matter. Come to think if it, I can't remember ever in my life having had any use for the little finger on my left hand . . ." So why shouldn't I bet him."

> ROALD DAHL
> "Man from the South" (1948)

Cupid and my Campaspe played
At cards for kisses

> JOHN LYLY (1553–1606)
> "Alexander and Campaspe"

JERRY "BABE" STEWART: All right . . . heads we do, tails we . . .
CONNIE: Get married!
JERRY: All right, I never go back on a coin.

> CLARK GABLE AND CAROLE LOMBARD
> in *No Man of Her Own* (1933)

One time he was sick and wouldn't take penicillin, because he bet his fever would go to one hundred and four.

FRANK SINATRA ON MARLON BRANDO
in Joseph L. Mankiewicz (screenwriter)
Guys and Dolls (1955)

———◆———

"Let's play for your mustache, Ergorov! That fluffy mustache of yours has bothered me for a long time. If I win, I'll cut off your mustache. Okay?"

MIKHAIL ZOSHCHENKO
"A Jolly Game" (1938)

———◆———

Four worthy Senators lately threw their hats into a river, laid a crown each whose hat should first swim to the mill, and ran hallooing after them; and he that won the prize, was in a greater rapture than if he had carried the most dangerous point in Parliament.

JOHN ASHTON
The History of Gambling in England (1898)

"I'll tell you what. I'll make you a little bet. Three times 35 is, er, 105. I'll bet you $105,000 you go to sleep before I do."

HUMPHREY BOGART
in John Huston (screenwriter)
The Treasure of the Sierra Madre (1948)

———◆———

The game had been hurriedly arranged so, in lieu of chips, they used buttons torn from their clothing.

ALLEN DOWLING
The Great American Pastime (1970)

———◆———

I got into a game with the mayor of some small town nearby and I remember he once asked me to jack the bet up and said if I didn't, he was gonna have me arrested for not gambling.

JIM REMPE
quoted in John Grissim, *Billiards* (1979)

———◆———

I hold you six to four that I love you with all my heart, if I would bet with other people I'm sure I could get ten to one.

JOHN WILMOT, EARL OF ROCHESTER (1647–80)
letter to his wife
Letters (1980)

Let us weight up the gain and loss involved in calling heads that God exists. Let us assess the two cases: if you win you win everything, if you lose nothing. Do not hesitate then; wager that he does exist.

> BLAISE PASCAL
> *Pensées* (1670)
> translated by Martin Turnell

———•◆•———

Duke Maximillian of Bavaria, playing billiards with his chamberlain Barthels, lost $3,600,000 in a single afternoon and was deposed as a result.

> ROBERT RIPLEY
> quoted in Robert Byrne, *Byrne's Wonderful World of Pool and Billiards* (1996)

———•◆•———

"I am the unluckiest guy in all the world. Here I am with a race that is a kick in the pants for my horse at fifty to one, and me without a quarter to bet. It is certainly a terrible thing to be poor," Hymie says. "Why," he says, "I will bet my life on my horse in this race, I am so sure of winning. I will bet my clothes. I will bet all I ever hope to have. In fact," he says, "I will even bet my ever-loving wife, this is how sure I am."

> DAMON RUNYON
> "The Ever-Loving Wife of Hymie's" (1934)

In 1933 Wilson Mizner lay dying. He was fifty-eight and all his life he had been a gamester. "Do you want a priest?" he was asked, during an interval of consciousness. "I want a priest, a rabbi and a Protestant clergyman," he managed to flash back. "I want to hedge my bets."

L. J. LUDOVICI
The Itch for Play (1962)

—————•◆•—————

1735. Oct. A child of James and Elizabeth Leesh of Chester le street, was played for at cards, at the sign of the Salmon, one game, four shillings against the child, by Henry and John Trotter, Robert Thomson and Thomas Ellison, which was won by the latter, and delivered to them accordingly.

LOCAL RECORDS, &C., OF REMARKABLE EVENTS
compiled by John Sykes (1824)

The feller took the box again, and took another long, particular look, and give it back to Smiley, and says, very deliberate, "Well," he says, "I don't see no p'ints about that frog that's any better'n any other frog."

"Maybe you don't," Smiley says. "Maybe you understand frogs and maybe you don't understand 'em; maybe you've had experience, and maybe you ain't only a amature, as it were. Anyways, I've got *my* opinion and I'll resk forty dollars that he can outjump any frog in Calaveras County."

MARK TWAIN
"The Notorious Jumping Frog of Calaveras County" (1865)

———— •◆• ————

If it was not horses it was crows. A crippled aunt, who could not get to the track, began the fashion of betting on which crow would leave a wall first. This proved so popular that the government considered putting a bounty on crows. In any case, soon after the time Gertie Garvin trained a pet crow, bird-gambling proved to be untrustworthy.

MICHAEL ONDAATJE
Running in the Family (1982)

At a classy Strip hotel the dice got really hot and action fast and furious. The lucky shooter became so excited stacking up $100 chips and throwing his winning dice that his false teeth fell out onto the green-felt table. The Boxman, without skipping a beat, whipped out his false teeth, and said, "You're faded."

MARIO PUZO
Inside Las Vegas (1976)

———◆———

I go to a party, I bet on the hors d'oeuvres.

BURT YOUNG
Lookin' to Get Out (1982)

———◆———

If there was two birds sitting on a fence, he would bet you which one would fly first.

MARK TWAIN
"The Notorious Jumping Frog of Calaveras Country" (1865)

There is a "game" some of the boys "play" in here called "playing the dozens." I have no idea what the origin of the name can be, but the idea is that the participants try to make each other mad by hurling epithets. The first one to lose his temper loses the game.

ALFRED HASSLER
Diary of a Self-Made Convict

———— •◆• ————

One that had play'd away even his Shirt and Cravat, and all his Clothes but his Breeches, stood shivering in the Corner of the Room, and another comforting him, and saying, *Damme* Jack, whoever thought to see thee in a State of Innocency.

SIR THOMAS BROWNE
quoted in John Ashton, *The History of Gambling in England* (1898)

———— •◆• ————

Kings themselves have been known to play off, at Primero, not only all the money and jewels they could part with, but the very images in the churches.

OLIVER GOLDSMITH (C. 1728–74)

Yudihishthira had gambled away all his possessions, including 100,000 slaves, 100,000 slave girls "adorned from head to foot," and finally his whole kingdom.

Even then Yudihishthira was unable to stop; he lost his brothers, himself, and, on the last throw of the dice, his wife Draupedi.

> Lyn Barrow
> *Compulsion* (1969)

———◆———

Then Draupadi cried out:—"Go you now and inquire whether Raja Yudihishthira lost me first or himself first; for if he played away himself first, he could not stake me."

> J. Talboys Wheeler
> *The History of India from the Earliest Ages* (1898)

———◆———

The natives are very great gamblers . . . they often gamble away houses, lands, canoes, and even the clothes off their backs.

> Peter Corney
> *Voyages in the Northern Pacific: Narrative of Several Trading Voyages from 1813–1818*

When Anne Boleyn and her fellow-accused were on trial, the odds in Tower Hall were ten to one on the acquittal of her brother Rochford because of his vigorous defense. In Abyssinia, betting on the sentence was a constant practice in the course of a legal session, and took place between the defense and the hearing of witnesses.

JOHAN HUIZINGA
Homo Ludens (1949)

———◆———

"One more play, Eddie. Everything I have on the red. I like red. It's the color of blood."

RAYMOND CHANDLER
The Big Sleep (1939)

———◆———

It's better in!

AMARILLO SLIM
calling a $51,000 raise

13

Lucky Thirteen

Gambling as a Model and Metaphor

Every conscious act requires risk. Every conscious act requires decision. Put these two facts together and you realize that the secret to life is not to avoid gambling, but to gamble well.

MIKE CARO
Mike Caro on Gambling (1984)

That man should be a gambler is but a natural outcome of the conditions of his existence. For is not the whole life of the individual a perpetual game, that is, a contest with universal nature, whose wily snares, strategems, and never-ending fierce attacks on, to get the better of him, he seeks to circumvent and avert?

CHARLES WILLIAM HECKETHORN
(ROUGE ET NOIR)
The Gambling World (1898)

G amble should be wholly voluntary and entered into with fair play—play that is fair, and play that is play. When we honor the spirit of gamble—as opposed to that of cheating, chiseling, or robbing a sucker—we agree with another to be subject to equal conditions, to be equals in relation to chance, or equals in our reliance on our own skills.

The just spirit of gamble makes none of the distinctions among race, gender, class, age, body types, those with disabilities, or any of the other ways in which humanity has been gaffing the wheel of fortune since anyone started keeping tabs. A pure honest gamble, heads or tails with an equally weighted two-sided coin, is as close to democratic fairness as humanity is likely to get, and the Greeks at times acknowledged this by electing officials through the drawing of lots. In this and many other ways gambling has been taken through the ages as a model for human institutions.

The sense of humanoids as ultimately subject to the same existential conditions—as guided in their careers on the planet by extraordinary accidents—has also made gambling into a widespread metaphor for life and death. In this long view of things, the games that humans play against each other are relatively low-stakes affairs in relation to the shoot-the-works games they play individually and collectively against the Nature of Things. The playful cynicism that seems always to have accompanied man's fateful sense of the contest with the universe as a losing proposition comes, no doubt, from the all-too-human sense of a cosmic and unyielding House percentage.

In *The Seventh Seal* (1957), director Ingmar Bergman gives the classic ponderous account of life as a chess game played against Death that Man is bound to lose in the end. In his brilliant spoof, "Death Knocks" (1971), Woody Allen recasts and restages Bergman's metaphor:

NAT: I'll play you gin rummy. If you win, I'll go immediately. If I win, give me some more time. A bit—one more day.
DEATH: Who's got time to play gin rummy?

When Death finally agrees, Nat suggests a little sweetening:

NAT: You want to play a tenth of a cent a point to make it interesting?
DEATH: It's not interesting enough for you?
NAT: I play better when money's at stake.

Needless to say, in Allen's version Death loses the day and has to borrow money from Nat for cab fare.

Nat will lose one of these days, but probably not tomorrow, and so he might as well enjoy one day at a time.

I like that version.

Fate is the player. We the counters are.
Heaven the dice, our earth the gaming board.

> IBN SINA
> quoted in Franz Rosenthal, *Gambling in Islam* (1975)

———•◆•———

"Here some one thrusts these cards into these old hands of mine; swears that I must play them, and no others."

> CAPTAIN AHAB
> in Herman Melville
> *Moby-Dick* (1851)

———•◆•———

All life is 6 to 5 against.

> SAM THE GONOPH
> in Damon Runyon
> "A Nice Price" (1931)

———•◆•———

Life is a gamble, at terrible odds—if it was a bet you wouldn't take it.

> TOM STOPPARD
> *Rosencrantz and Guilderstern Are Dead* (1967)

In the struggle between you and the world second the world.

> FRANZ KAFKA (1883–1924)
> *Aphorisms*

———— •◆• ————

He was too much of a gambler not to accept fate. With him life was at best an uncertain game, and he recognized the usual percentage in favor of the dealer.

> BRET HARTE
> "The Outcasts of Poker Flat" (1870)

———— •◆• ————

Life is only a game of poker, played well or ill;
Some hold four aces, some draw or fill;
Some make a bluff and oft get there,
While others ante and never hold a pair.

> PAT HOGAN
> on the back of an ace of hearts found among his effects,
> quoted in Robert K. DeArment, *Knights of the Green Cloth* (1892)

The most fundamental principle of all in gambling is simply equal conditions . . . To the extent to which you depart from that equality, if it is in your opponent's favor, you are a fool, and if in your own, you are unjust.

GEROLAMO CARDANO
The Book on Games of Chance (c. 1520)

———•◆•———

When his palm gets hold of the dice,
The rich man is (no better than) a pauper in his company.

AL-IMAD AL-ISFAHANI
quoted in Franz Rosenthal, *Gambling in Islam* (1975)

———•◆•———

At the gaming-table all men are equal; no superiority of birth, accomplishments, or ability avail here; great noble-men, merchants, orators, jockeys, statesmen, and idlers are here thrown together.

CHARLES GREVILLE
Memoirs (1874)

———•◆•———

Gambling is the great leveller. All men are equal at cards.

NIKOLAI GOGOL
The Gamblers (1842)
translated by Alexander Berkman

Your money is as good as anybody else's money, and it doesn't come fairer than that, or more democratic.

> MICHAEL HERR
> on casinos
> *The Big Room* (1986)

———•◆•———

The dice of God are always loaded.

> GREEK PROVERB

———•◆•———

I shall never believe that God plays dice with the world.

> ALBERT EINSTEIN
> quoted in Phillip Frank, *Einstein, His Life and Times* (1953)

———•◆•———

It seems hard to sneak a look at God's cards. But that he plays dice and uses "telepathic" methods (as the present quantum theory requires of him) is something that I cannot believe for a single moment.

> ALBERT EINSTEIN
> letter to Lanczos (1942)

God not only plays dice. He also sometimes throws the dice where they cannot be seen.

> STEPHEN HAWKING
> *Nature* (vol. 257)

———•◆•———

If the metaphysician does not actually play with loaded dice, he often uses dice which he has never examined, and which, for all he knows, may have been marked rightly or wrongly by those who placed them in his hands.

> MAX MULLER (1823–1900)

———•◆•———

Keeping vigil
  doubting
    rolling
      shining and meditating

Before coming to a halt
at some terminus that satisfies it

All thought emits a throw of the dice

> STÉPHANE MALLARMÉ
> "A Throw of the Dice Can Never Abolish Chance" (1897)
> translated by Henry Weinfield

An *Ace* of *Hearts* steps forth; The *King,* unseen,
Lurk'd in her Hand, and mourn'd his captive *Queen.*
He springs to Vengeance with an eager Pace,
And falls like Thunder on the prostrate *Ace.*

ALEXANDER POPE
"The Rape of the Lock" (1712)

When I see the Ace, it reminds me that there is only
    one God.
When I see the Deuce, it reminds me of the Father and
    the Son.
When I see the Tray, it reminds me of the Father, Son
    and Holy Ghost.
When I see the Four, it reminds me of the four
    Evangelists that preached, viz., Matthew,
    Mark, Luke and John.

RICHARD MIDDLETON
The Perpetual Almanack, or Soldier's Prayer Book (1744)

All voting is a sort of gaming, like chequers or backgammon, with a slight moral twinge to it, a playing with right and wrong, with moral questions; and betting naturally accompanies it.

HENRY DAVID THOREAU
Civil Disobedience (1849)

———•◆•———

When I was young, people called me a gambler. As the scale of my operations increased I became known as a speculator. Now I am called a banker. But I have been doing the same thing all the time.

SIR ERNEST CASSEL, PRIVATE BANKER TO EDWARD VII
quoted in John Ashton, *The History of Gambling* (1898)

———•◆•———

Gambling promises the poor what property performs for the rich—something for nothing.

GEORGE BERNARD SHAW (1856–1959)

———•◆•———

The gambling known as business looks with austere disfavor upon the business known as gambling.

AMBROSE BIERCE
The Devil's Dictionary (1906)

Mountains of gold were in a few moments reduced to nothing at once part of the table, and rose as suddenly in another. The rich grew in a moment poor, and the poor as suddenly became rich; so that it seemed a philosopher could nowhere have so well instructed his pupils in the contempt of riches, at least he could nowhere have better inculcated the uncertainty of their duration.

HENRY FIELDING
Tom Jones (1749)

I have indeed now and then a little compunction in reflecting that I spend time so idly; but another reflection comes to relieve me, whispering, '*you know that that soul is immortal; why then should you be such a niggard of a little time, when you have a whole eternity before you?*' So, being easily convinced, and, like other reasonable creatures, satisfied with a small reason, when it is in favour of doing what I have a mind to, I shuffle the cards again, and begin another game.

BEN FRANKLIN
letter to Mrs. Hewson (Polly Stevenson; May 1786)

Nanny was lying very still. Then she looked up and whispered to Mrs Heta:

—Maka . . . Maka tiko bum . . . I want a game of cards . . .

A pack of cards was found. The old ladies sat around the bed, playing. Everybody else decided to play cards too . . . The men played poker in the kitchen and sitting room. The kids played snap . . . The house overflowed with card players, even onto the lawn outside Nanny's window, where she could see.

WITI IHIMAERA
"A Game of Cards" (1972)

His very appearance seemed to say: "In no way can the incident of this funeral service for Ivan Ilyich be considered sufficient grounds for canceling the regular session; that is, nothing can prevent us from meeting tonight and flipping through a new deck of cards while a footman places four fresh candles around the table. There is, in fact, no reason to assume this incident can keep up from a pleasant evening."

LEO TOLSTOY
"The Death of Ivan Ilyich" (1886)

"Let us play," an American friend of mine sometimes says, "we shall be a long time dead."

CHARLES WILLIAM HECKETHORN (ROUGE ET NOIR)
The Gambling World (1898)

The tick-ticking of the casino's money wheel, first accelerating rapidly and then taking forever to slowly come to a stop, each click lingering slightly longer in the ear than the previous one until the final surprising eternal *ick,* which merely produces another in an endless series of spins.

JOHN O'BRIEN
Leaving Las Vegas (1990)

Came to play, not to stay.

POPULAR SAYING

Now dealer and players alike united in an unspoken conspiracy to stave off morning forever . . . For the cards kept the everlasting darkness off, the cards lent everlasting hope.

NELSON ALGREN
The Man with the Golden Arm (1949)

Soon fades the spell, soon comes the night;
Say will it not be then the same,
Whether we played the black or white,
Whether we won or lost the game?

THOMAS BABINGTON MACAULAY (1801–59)

———•◆•———

We all know the condition of life's game. The Big Dealer sets a time limit for each of us.

HAROLD S. SMITH SR. WITH JOHN WESLEY NOBLE
I Want to Quit Winners (1961)

———•◆•———

It is only at the end that I will know what I have finally lost or won in this huge casino where I have spent sixty years, cup in hand.

DENIS DIDEROT (1713–84)

———•◆•———

At the age of seventy-nine, she was told that an operation was necessary to save her life, and it was doubtful that she would recover . . . with a gambler's viewpoint she said, "Go ahead. I've bucked worse odds than that, and I've always hated a piker."

NOLIE NUMEY
Poker Alice (1951)

You can't beat death, taxes, and percentages.

> NICK "THE GREEK" DANDALOS
> quoted in Cy Rice, *Nick the Greek: King of Gamblers* (1969)

———— ◆ ————

Death and dice level all distinctions.

> SAMUEL FOOTE (1720–77)

———— ◆ ————

What ho! Bring dice and good wine
Who cares for the morrow?
Live—so calls grinning death—
Live, for I come to you soon.

> VIRGIL
> *Eclogues* (43–37 B.C.)

———— ◆ ————

NAT: Hello, Moe? Me. Listen, I don't know if somebody's playing a joke, or what, but Death was just here. We played a little gin . . . No, *Death*. In person. Or somebody who claims to be Death. But, Moe, he's such a *schlep!*

> WOODY ALLEN
> *Death Knocks* (1971)

Should I go to heaven, give me no haloed angels riding
snow-white clouds . . . Give me rather a vaulting red-walled
casino with bright lights, bring on horned devils as dealers.
Let there be a Pit Boss in the Sky who will give me unlimited
credit. And if there is a merciful God in our Universe he will
decree that the Player have for *all* eternity, an Edge against
the House.

MARIO PUZO
Inside Las Vegas (1976)

Best Bets:

A Few of My Favorite Writings about Gambling

For the most part gamblers are silver-tongued talkers, but tin-eared writers (if they write at all). Even Minnesota Fats, who claimed to have won two world speaking titles in Canada alone, published his book "with" the help of professional writer Tom Fox. Gamblers too often write to pay off markers, or to boast about their achievements and belittle rivals, or to market their expertise (sometimes in manuals on "how-to-beat-the-slots" that amount to little more than scams from a safe distance).

Writing is itself part gamble, and when writers pick up a cue or roll the dice they hedge their bets that through writing about it they can redeem their gambling, cover or justify their time and expense. Most of the authors of the texts recommended below, one suspects, are skalds with "ears" (or tape recorders) in the great tradition of writer-spongers like

Nelson Agren ("the bard of stumblebum"), Bret Harte ("the Homer of gamblers"), and Damon Runyon ("official diarist of New York after dark"), who peppered their fictions with the quips of anonymous gamblers.

What justifies any writer's scamming of phrases, whatever the subject, is insight. As with good gambling, this is achieved only through discipline and feel for the subject, understanding of psychology and situation, attentiveness to detail, and imaginative daring. Happily for readers, writers are people who, having achieved insights (however dubious), cannot or choose not to play their cards close to their vests.

Fiction

Frederick Barthelme, *Bob the Gambler* (1997)
Barthelme's novel follows down-on-his-luck architect Ray Kaiser, nicknamed "Bob the Gambler" by his daughter (after *Bob le Flambeur,* the great French gambling film, 1955), from his first slot thrills with his wife to over-the-falls sessions at the blackjack table. The scenes describing his visceral emotions as he gambles are superb, and striking for the ways that, even in the moment of defeat, they acknowledge the thrill of the ride. A *New Yorker* article, written with brother Steven (titled "Good Losers," March 1999), gives a

frank, insightful, and unapologetic account of their costly immersion in gamble.

Fyodor Dostoevsky, *The Gambler* (1867)

Dostoevsky's renowned novel about a man's fascination and compulsion at the roulette table was dictated to his future long-suffering wife, Anna, in three weeks to pay off debts. Dostoevsky had high stakes in finishing quickly: If he did not deliver the manuscript on time his publisher would assume the rights to Dostoevsky's earlier books. When it looked like Dostoevsky would finish on time the publisher left town for the weekend, but Anna had the manuscript taken to the police station and notarized. Among the many gambling works influenced by Dostoevsky's novel is the film *The Gambler* (1974), written by James Toback, in which James Caan plays compulsive gambler and Columbia professor Axel Freed (who of course lectures on Dostoevsky).

Richard Jessup, *The Cincinnati Kid* (1963)

Despite the improbable final hand of the showdown between the Kid and Lancey (i.e., Lancey would have folded before drawing out), this novel is the acknowledged classic among poker novels. In his introduction to the 1985 edition, Jerome Charyn captures some of the book's lasting appeal: "We're all players of one sort or another . . . There's always a Lancey out there to steal our pants and destroy our most secret desires. Defeated like the Cincinnati Kid, we wait, wait, wait until the dream comes back to us, a bit at a time." Card players will also continue to appreciate the book for its brilliant attention to the details of card rituals. Norman Jewison directed a worthy film version of the book, starring Steve McQueen as the Kid and Edward G. Robinson as Lancey (1965).

Walter Tevis, *The Hustler* (1959), *The Color of Money* (1984)
Perhaps no single writer has done more for his sport than Tevis did for pool with his two novels centering on Fast Eddie Felson's pursuit of excellence on the green felt. Felson pays for his mistakes, on and off the table, but for Tevis he is defined, like any artist, by his ability to perform what he imagines. Tevis's dramatic descriptions of pool games as they unfold, of drawn-out sessions that test the pool-player-as-artist's character and creativity, are unmatched. Taken as a sequence, the two books show both transformations in the world of pool and poolhalls, and continuities in the essential terms of the game itself. Paul Newman and Jackie Gleason play Fast Eddie and Fats in the classic film version of *The Hustler* (1961), and Newman (in an Academy Award–winning performance) returns alongside Tom Cruise in *The Color of Money* (1986).

Nonfiction/Memoir

Alvin Alvarez, *The Biggest Game in Town* (1983)
I first came across Alvarez's writing in an elegant, erudite book on John Donne in a course on metaphysical poetry; imagine my delight in bumping into him again in a *New Yorker* essay ("No Limit," 1994) where his scholarly attentiveness was trained upon the World Series of Poker. *The Biggest Game in Town* records, at book length, how Alvarez's love of poker brought him to Vegas for the annual championship, where he met and interviewed poker greats including Amarillo Slim, Pug Pearson, and Johnny Moss, and got his feet wet at world-class poker as well.

Jon Bradshaw, *Fast Company* (1975)
Journalist Bradshaw brings his investigative skills together with his passion for gambling in this series of partial profiles of famous American gamblers in their "natural environments": The book includes a generous helping of quotations from interviews with poker champions Pug Pearson and Johnny Moss, tennis impresario Bobby Riggs, pool player-talker Minnesota Fats, backgammon champion Tim Holland, and golf and proposition-bet artist Titanic Thompson.

John Grissim, *Billiards: Hustlers & Heroes, Legends & Lies and the Search for Higher Truth on the Green Felt* (1979)
Every bit up to its title, this ebullient celebration of the game is rich in anecdote and poolosophy (including Zen billiards, "zilliards"). Grissim's compendium includes lower truths as well, along with interviews with pool players and hustlers, sidebars on tournaments and particular games and pool legends, historical information about the development of the game, and accounts of the author's own misadventures on the table.

Anthony Holden, *Big Deal: One Year as a Professional Poker Player* (1995)
Although it appeared only a few years ago, this odyssey of an English writer (and "crony" of Alvarez's), who ventures away from his Tuesday-night poker game and into the unsparing world of professional poker for a year, is cited frequently in texts about poker. This is no doubt in some part because Holden is such good company as he describes poker personalities, the tension of individual games, and his ideas about gambling and the gambler's life, and in large part because Holden appeals to that side of every serious recreational player who dreams of one day sitting down with the best, a fantasy well expressed in the recent film *Rounders* (1998), which starred

Matt Damon and John Malkovich (whose deliciously unlikely tell is twisting an Oreo cookie next to his ear).

David McCumber, *Off the Rail: A Pool Hustler's Journey* (1996)
Journeyman writer David McCumber, who had edited Hunter Thompson and others, takes the reader on a yearlong road trip in pursuit of action with professional pool player Tony Annigoni, whom McCumber stakes in part with his advance money. McCumber catches the rhythm of road action, with its dull spaces, quick-developing risks, and dramatic showdowns and ego clashes, whether in high-stakes tournament rooms or dicey dives.

Dan McGoorty as told to Robert Byrne, *McGoorty: A Billiard Hustler's Life* (1972)
Robert Byrne, a national-class cueman who has written many excellent books about all aspects of the game of pool, makes the perfect recorder for Dan McGoorty's recollections of a lifetime of hustling billiards. It is a story that spans the Golden Age of pool, packed with remembrances of personalities and places, lean years hoboing around and drinking, playing with nothing but nerve in his pocket. Of his frank, sometimes bitter stories, McGoorty told Byrne, "If what I told you got published they'd lock us up for life. I tell the truth you know."

Mario Puzo, *Inside Las Vegas* (1976)
Full of savvy cut-to-the-chase statements and witty anecdotes about gambling and its varied history, Puzo's unabashed paean to Vegas catches the gambling mecca's glitter and lyric sordidness. The best-selling author of *The Godfather* and a self-proclaimed recent ex-"degenerate" gambler (at the time), Puzo's street-corner wit and wisdom make the book a gambler's delight.

Jack Richardson, *Memoir of a Gambler* (1979)
A suave, carnal, existential picaresque through the underside of the gambling world from Las Vegas to Macao. Richardson, an acclaimed playwright and a longtime columnist for *Esquire* on gambling, is a true scholar of squalor, a brilliant self-diagnostician, and a memorable storyteller.

Herbert O. Yardley, *Education of a Poker Player: Including Where and How One Learns to Win* (1970)
About this book, considered by many to be "the bible," Alvarez wrote Holden, "When I first picked it up I was ignorant not only in the ways of poker. I also had the deep ignorance which goes with excessive education." In addition to containing how-to and life-lesson materials potentially helpful to academics with overcoming naïveté (if not improving their poker), the book is tremendously entertaining in its

accounts of Yardley's own education at Monty's Poker Parlor, and his passing along of that information during his days as a cryptographer in Asia. In an age of poker printouts and computer analysis, this earthy book remains one of the best manuals for learning basic poker strategy.

Personal Essays

Stephen Dunn, "Gambling: Remembrances and Assertions" in *Walking Light* (1993)
Poet Stephen Dunn describes an essayist as "a person who believes there's value in being overheard clarifying things for himself." Dunn begins his attempt at clarifying his lifelong fascinating with gambling with remembrances of early gambling in his household, and then moves on to measured assertions about the great gambler's mixtures of knowing and daring. For Dunn the gambler, rightly seen, emerges finally as someone willing to accept the costs of gambling for the chances it affords him to be "startled or enlarged."

David Mamet, "Things I Have Learned Playing Poker on the Hill" in *Writing in Restaurants* (1986)
In his plays Mamet presents gamblers and gambling with a clean, cold, philosophical edge—he focuses on the character of gamblers, con artists, and salesmen who read their

opponents' characters through their tells (see in particular *House of Games,* 1987). In this essay, which draws on years of experience in a weekly poker game, Mamet gives a brilliant and intimate diagnosis of the gambler's relation to games, losing, and luck, among other things.

Anthologies

Annabel Davis-Goff (editor), *The Literary Companion to Gambling* (1996)
The best "literary" anthology of gambling writing that I've come across. Davis-Goff presents scenes and selections, most no longer than a few pages, all by writers famous for their non-gambling writings as well. The arrangement of the book into sections entitled "Gods," "Man," and "Self," with the selections ranging from the ancient to the contemporary, makes the anthology read like an extended meditation on the transformations and continuities in the human love affair with gambling.

Robert Byrne (editor), *Byrne's Book of Great Pool Stories* (1995)
A fine selection of thirty-one short stories about pool, billiards, and snooker, including works by Leo Tolstoy, A. A. Milne, Saki, Wallace Stegner, and Walter Tevis. The stories capture a range of pool scenes, from the sublime of a well-played match

to the compulsiveness of a match continued during cannon fire to a man with nothing left to wager but his mustache.

How-to-Win Books

Beginning with mathematician Edward O. Thorp's *Beat the Dealer* (1962), the best-selling book on card counting as a way to give the player an edge over the House in blackjack, instructional manuals have become increasingly technical. There are now fascinatingly complex computer analyses (i.e., neural-network rollouts) available on every aspect of gambling, which circulate mainly among professionals, and would be about as amusing as actuarial charts to nonspecialists. For general readers, the works of gambling authors such as Frank Scoblete (casino games), Paul Magriel (backgammon), Andrew Beyer (horse racing), Ken Uston (blackjack), Mike Caro and Bobby Baldwin (poker and gambling), Avery Cardoza (poker and casino games), Darwin Ortiz (casino gambling), Robert Byrne, Phil Capelle, and Steve Mizerak (pool and billiards) all offer less daunting professional advice. Anyone considering venturing outside of their friendly, weekly poker game had better read Doyle Brunson's *How I Made $1,000,000 Playing Poker,* a compendium of poker essays with discussions of individual games by champions Bobby Baldwin, Mike Caro, Joey Hawthorne, David "Chip" Reese, and David Sklansky (as told to Allan Goldberg), Herbert O. Yardley's *Education* mentioned above, and A. D. Livingston's *Poker Strategy and Winning Play*. Blackjack players would profitably begin with *The Gambling Times Guide to Blackjack,* by Stanley Roberts with Edward O. Thorp, Ken Uston, Lance Humble, Arnold Snyder, Julian Braun, D. Howard Mitchell, Jerry Patterson, and other blackjack experts, and Lance Humble, Ph.D., and Carl Cooper, Ph.D., *The World's Greatest Blackjack Book*. Football bettors would enjoy Larry Merchant's memoir of a year of gridiron handicapping, *The National Football Lottery.*

Selected Academic Bibliography

History

Herbert Asbury, *Sucker's Progress: An Informal History of Gambling in America from the Colonies to Canfield* (1938)

John Ashton, *The History of Gambling in England* (1898)

Robert K. DeArment, *Knights of the Green Cloth: The Saga of the Frontier Gamblers* (1892)

Allen Dowling, *The Great American Pastime* (1970)

John M. Findlay, *People of Chance: Gambling in American Society from Jamestown to Las Vegas* (1986)

Alice Fleming, *Something for Nothing: A History of Gambling* (1978)

Mike Shamos, *Pool: History, Strategies, and Legends* (1994)

Alan Wykes, *The Complete Illustrated Guide to Gambling* (1964)

Anthropology/Sociology

Roger Caillois, *Man, Play, and Games* (1979)

Sigmund Freud, "Dostoevsky and Parricide" (1928)

Clifford Geertz, "Deep Play: Notes on the Balinese Cockfight" (1972)

Irving Goffman, *Where the Action Is* (1967)

Johan Huizinga, *Homo Ludens* (1949)

Ned Polsky, *Hustlers, Beats, and Others* (Updated, 1998)

Index of Authors and Works Cited

INDEX OF AUTHORS AND WORKS CITED